SHAKING THE HEAVENS

ANA MÉNDEZ

A Division of Gospel Light
Ventura, California, U.S.A.

Published by Renew Books
A Division of Gospel Light
Ventura, California, U.S.A.
Printed in the U.S.A.

Renew Books is a ministry of Gospel Light, an evangelical Christian publisher dedicated to serving the local church. We believe God's vision for Gospel Light is to provide church leaders with biblical, user-friendly materials that will help them evangelize, disciple and minister to children, youth and families.

It is our prayer that this Renew book will help you discover biblical truth for your own life and help you meet the needs of others. May God richly bless you.

For a free catalog of resources from Renew Books and Gospel Light, please call your Christian supplier or contact us at 1-800-4-GOSPEL *or* www.regalbooks.com.

Cover Design by Kevin Keller
Internal Design by Robert Williams

Library of Congress Cataloging-in-Publication Data
Méndez, Ana, 1954-
Shaking the heavens / Ana Méndez.
p. cm.
ISBN 0-8307-2496-6
1. Spiritual warfare. I. Title.
BV4509.5 .M46 2001
235'.4—dc21 00-062626

1 2 3 4 5 6 7 8 9 10 11 12 13 14 15 / 05 04 03 02 01 00

I dedicate this book to my beloved heavenly Father, my Lord and Savior Jesus Christ and the Holy Spirit, who truly inspired it . . . and to my apostle and personal pastor, Dr. Rony Chaves, whose ministry and support God used to give me the anointing, the wisdom and the courage to understand and do the spiritual warfare in the dimensions described in this book.

CONTENTS

Part One: It Is a Time of War

Part Two: Territorial Warfare

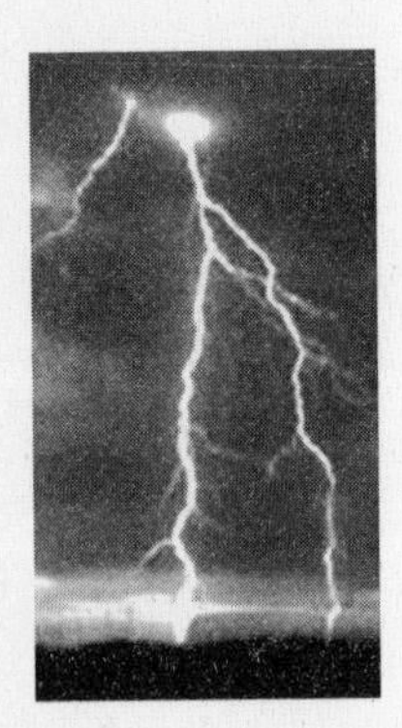

FOREWORD

The Church today has been placed in an extraordinary position. Our transition into the twenty-first century reminds me of the Allied forces and their position after the Battle of the Bulge in World War II. When the news came that the Allies had won that intense and costly battle, we all knew it was just a matter of time until the war in Europe would be over. Adolf Hitler would certainly be defeated. Yet at that point the Nazis still possessed tremendous military might, and we knew the rest of the war would not be easy. We expected many more casualties on both sides. Still, we did not know how long it would take; but we did know one thing—we were going to win!

The Church has been engaged in warfare against the kingdom of darkness since day one. We've known some great victories: the conversion of Europe, the Protestant Reformation, the Wesleyan revival, the modern missionary movement, to name a few. We have also known setbacks: the spread of Islam across

North Africa and 70 years of atheistic Communism in many parts of the world, for example. But for every step back, the Church took two steps forward. This was very much the experience of the Allies as they pushed the Axis powers back across North Africa, landed on Normandy on D-day, fought bitterly into Belgium and won the Battle of the Bulge in 1944.

The past decade of spiritual warfare was not easy. As God's people moved against positions the enemy has held for millennia, Satan counterattacked ferociously. But the Church rose to the occasion, and nowhere in the pages of Church history do we find Christians engaging the devil in spiritual warfare with such intensity, with such determination and with such newly revealed weaponry as in recent years. God has entrusted His Church with combat assignments in the invisible world on levels higher than anything we have record of in the past. And as the past millennium came to a close, I personally felt that we had won the spiritual Battle of the Bulge.

One of the spiritual generals whom God has called forth to lead the troops into battle is Ana Méndez. I use the term "generals" advisedly, because I realize that large armies have relatively few generals. The same is true in the segment of the worldwide Body of Christ that I am in touch with today. Every member of the army of God is extremely important, from the foot soldiers to the very top officers; but if the army is going to be victorious, leadership is crucial. Ana Méndez is one of those leaders who sees the whole picture, who hears from God and receives directions, who motivates the troops to go into battle, who draws up the battle plans and who fights on the front lines herself.

Not every general can be found on the front lines. General Dwight D. Eisenhower, for example, logged no time in a foxhole at the Battle of the Bulge, nor did he fire a single shot. There is, of course, nothing wrong with Eisenhower's decision to lead from a distance. But this is not how Ana Méndez sees her role in spiritual warfare. Ana has warred in the Himalayas on Mount Everest itself. She has battled in the upper regions of the Nile River. She located what may be the original site of the Garden of Eden in Turkey and there built a symbolic altar to the glory of God. She has confronted the powers of darkness in piranha-infested lagoons in the headwaters of the Amazon, and she has anointed with oil the ancient trade route between Egypt and Israel. These were just a few of her demanding front-line assignments from the Lord.

While we have won a major battle in recent years, the war is not over. There is no question that the victory is ours, because we serve no less than the King of kings and the Lord of lords. However, this is no time for either the generals or the foot soldiers to retire. God is calling forth many more soldiers and many more officers. And we have an excellent plan for the battle.

Ana Méndez has done us all a favor by writing down the insights, the experiences, the revelation and the strategies for spiritual warfare that God has given her. The book that you hold in your hands is a map of the front lines of spiritual warfare for many days to come.

My prayer is that as you read *Shaking the Heavens*, you will become prepared to move to a new level in your service to God. You will be blessed!

C. PETER WAGNER
Chancellor, Wagner Leadership Institute

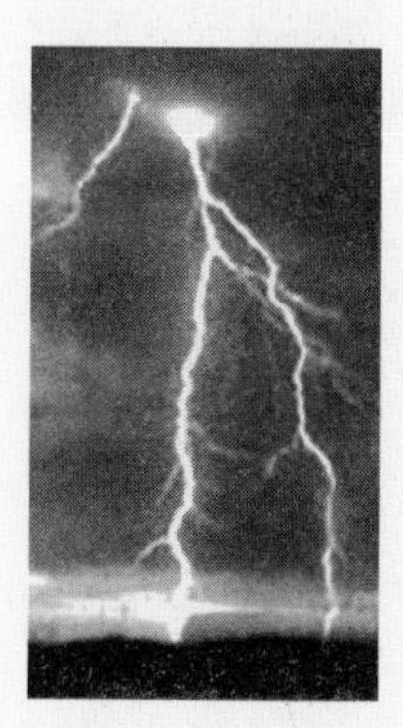

PROLOGUE

A new wave of the Holy Spirit is flooding the earth today with a powerful emphasis on spiritual warfare. The Lord of hosts is preparing His people to bring about Satan's greatest defeat in modern times.

The Living Word is pouring forth great revelation from the divine throne, equipping the teachers of the Church to impart this simple, practical and, at the same time, very deep knowledge to every believer. It is the Father's longing to make every one of His children a true spiritual warrior, armed and prepared to carry out the work of intercession effectively and in power. Hallelujah!

Today, a powerful, warlike anointing is filling the Church as the Lord leads us into battle against demonic powers. God is definitively on the offensive, and He is rousing us to engage in strategic spiritual warfare against Satan and his forces.

This book by Ana Méndez comes at an opportune time—God's timing—and it springs forth like a river in the middle of a desert. Very little reliable material has been printed on the subject of spiritual warfare, leaving an age-old void in the life and spiritual growth of the Church.

Ana comes out of a life of voodoo and witchcraft, from which she was saved and transformed by the grace of God. Today she is a fervent intercessor—a true spiritual warrior in prayer. She has much to teach us.

The anointing which has been won by this woman of prayer in battle makes this an important work and one which should be read with rapt attention. As a prophet of God, I dare to assure you that once you have read it, you will never be the same. You, too, will be enlisted by the Holy Spirit into God's army.

DR. RONY CHAVES

PART ONE

IT IS A TIME OF WAR

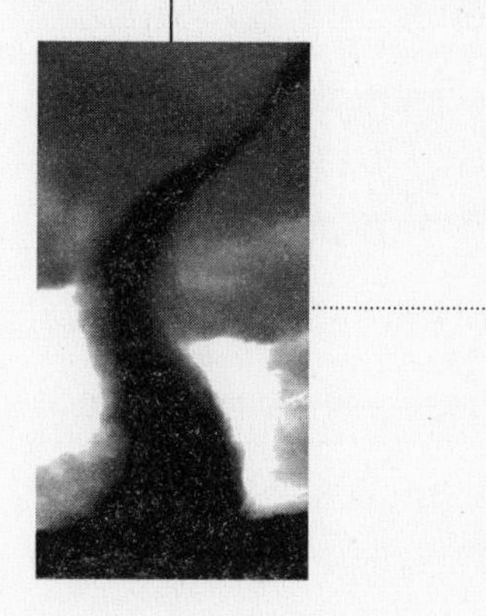

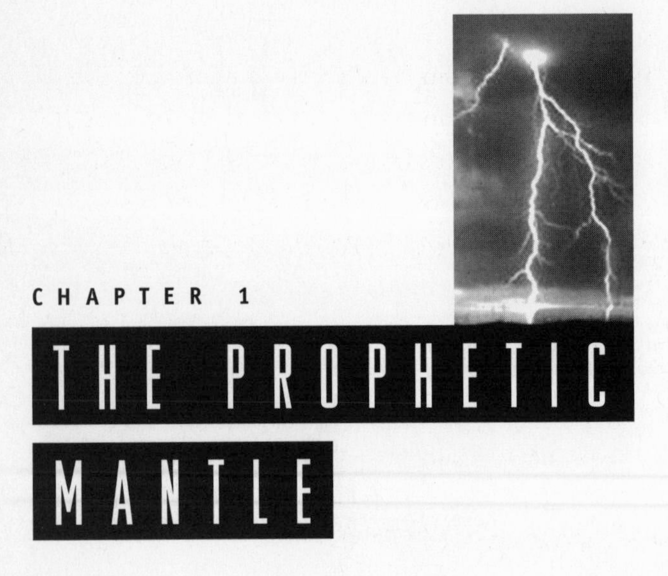

CHAPTER 1
THE PROPHETIC MANTLE

Since the time of Martin Luther, God has progressively unfolded for the Church a revelation of warfare in the heavenlies. This outpouring of His light, age after age, has come in the form of diverse cycles of understanding of His Word.

Today, He has already begun the last of these cycles with a move of such magnitude that it will lead the Church to its greatest expression of His glory. This move of the Holy Spirit will unleash the latter rain, dressing the Bride of the Lamb in the splendor of holiness and purity and adorning her with gold and precious stones, which are the righteous deeds of the saints. This move will raise up the victorious army of God with such a powerful manifestation of the Holy Spirit so as to subdue all the enemies of Jesus Christ under His footstool.

A study of biblical prophecy reveals that Scripture is as concerned with the timing of events to come as it is with the events themselves. It is essential that we be aware of the times in which we live:

> When you see a cloud rising in the west, immediately you say, "It's going to rain," and it does. And when the south wind blows, you say, "It's going to be hot," and it is. Hypocrites! You know how to interpret the appearance of the earth and sky. How is it that you don't know how to interpret this present time? (Luke 12:54-56).

Ours is a cultural and spiritual environment ripe for earthly and spiritual events foretold in the pages of the Bible long ago, and this same environment is allowing us to move in God's will in our generation.

The Spirit of God moved His servant Daniel to study the prophecy given to Jeremiah in a personal letter years earlier. It was revealed to Daniel that after the 70 years had been completed (foretold by Jeremiah), the Babylonian captivity would end, for the time had come to return to Jerusalem. Upon learning this, Daniel entered into a profound fast and a powerful time of intercession that helped to bring about the deliverance of his people in accordance with the prophecy. Daniel understood his time!

Today, God is waking the spirits of thousands of His people and depositing within them a revelation of His plans and strategies for these final days. "Surely the Sovereign LORD does nothing without revealing his plan to his servants the prophets" (Amos 3:7). This is a people anointed by God to understand the times in which we are living. As God roused the spirits of Cyrus,

Ezra, Nehemiah and Zerubbabel to reconstruct the Temple and the walls of Jerusalem, God is today sounding a trumpet so loudly that the ears of His people hear the voice of the Almighty and are able to clearly distinguish it from the insistent, destructive murmurs of the enemy.

A prophetic anointing, an anointing of spiritual discernment, an anointing of wisdom and a powerful anointing of spiritual warfare are being released over the Church of Jesus Christ. This is a time of manifestation and demonstration, a time of fulfillment, a time of revelation, a time in which we are already seeing the things many previous generations desired to see but which God has granted to us, a chosen generation. This time, chosen by God, will precede the coming of our Lord, Jesus Christ, in all His power and glory!

Our generation shall see the greatest movement of restoration in history, for it is written of Christ and His return, "Whom heaven must receive [and retain] until the time for the complete restoration of all that God spoke by the mouth of all His holy prophets for ages past [from the most ancient time in the memory of man]" (Acts 3:21, *AMP*). This time of restoration will culminate with His return to establish His reign, His throne and the supreme and absolute authority of God over everything created, as it was in the beginning.

A Time for Shaking

Now is a time of profound alertness and the laying of spiritual foundations. It is also a time of shaking, as written in the epistle to the Hebrews:

> At that time his voice shook the earth, but now he has promised, "Once more I will shake not only the earth but also the heavens." The words "once more" indicate the removing of what can be shaken—that is, created things—so that what cannot be shaken may remain (Heb. 12:26,27).

Everything that can be removed—the false foundations upon which the world has placed its trust, the glory of man, the strongholds of sin, worldly kingdoms and structures, the devil and his kingdom—will be removed for the establishing of the only stable, unshakable, perfect things: (1) the kingdom of God and (2) the Word which has proceeded from the mouth of God (see Matt. 24:35).

Now is the time of which the Lord prophesied:

> There will be signs in the sun, moon and stars. On the earth, nations will be in anguish and perplexity at the roaring and tossing of the sea. Men will faint from terror, apprehensive of what is coming on the world, *for the heavenly bodies will be shaken*. Be always on the watch, and pray that you may be able to escape all that is about to happen, and that you may be able to stand before the Son of Man (Luke 21:25,26,36, emphasis added).

God is raising up people who are alert in order to loose upon them a spirit of spiritual warfare to pull down the strongholds of the devil. Earthquakes and other signs of the last days are accompanied by a growing army of God's people equipped with the knowledge that He is shaking, removing and tearing down the infernal foundations in the heavenly places. God has spoken:

> Raise a banner on a bare hilltop, shout to them; beckon to them to enter the gates of the nobles. I have commanded my holy ones; I have summoned my warriors to carry out my wrath—those who rejoice in my triumph. Listen, a noise on the mountains, like that of a great multitude! Listen, an uproar among the kingdoms, like nations massing together! The LORD Almighty is mustering an army for war (Isa. 13:2-4).

Church, it is a time of war, it is a time of victory!

This is a time of intense divine activity, as we are entering an age of escalating confrontation between the kingdom of God and the kingdom of darkness. The most glorious manifestation of God's power upon the Church is before us: the all-powerful covering of the mantle of God's glory with which He will clothe Christ's betrothed one.

A Time of Attack

Simultaneously, the enemy is launching the most violent, aggressive and destructive attack the Body of Christ has ever suffered. Satan is unleashing his hosts in a last-ditch assault designed to finally bring about mankind's destruction. Spirits of depression, discouragement, fear, intimidation, witchcraft, sorcery, division, malice and slander are being launched to pull down leaders and break up churches. Never before have we seen so many faithful servants in Christian congregations turning away, so many pastors falling, so many families breaking up and so many believers apostatizing.

What is happening? That which the Bible has prophesied: these last days will be characterized by apostasy. Because of the increase of wickedness, the love of most will grow cold. There is a shout in the heavens crying out to us in earnest warning: *Time is running out!* Even the chosen, if possible, will be deceived; and if the times were not cut short, nobody could be saved (see Matt. 24:22).

I have seen whole churches destroyed, because they did not know how to be in a state of alert; there were no watchmen on the walls. Like a progressive, deadly infection, I witnessed indolence, permissiveness, sin, gossip and dissension enter the doors of these churches; and nobody was brave enough to speak against it.

One day while I was praying for the Church, the Lord caused His Spirit to come upon me, taking me inside God's heart. I started to groan as I had never done before. I was in divine sorrow, crying the same tears God was crying for his people.

We have entered into the most powerful movement of the Spirit of God in history—the last prophetic cycle—and Satan has responded by filling hearts with complacency, conformity and laziness. We are allowing ourselves to be carried away by lustful desires and pleasures of this world. It is written: "For although they knew God, they neither glorified him as God nor gave thanks to him, but their thinking became futile and their foolish hearts were darkened. Although they claimed to be wise, they became fools" (Rom. 1:21,22).

God's people are sleeping while the heart of God is weeping.

God is groaning, for the heavens have been opened over many nations, and He is pouring out His fire upon the Church to raise it up in majesty—and yet so many of His people continue to slumber.

He groans because He is not going to change his timing, not even for the intense pain He experiences on seeing us asleep.

The trumpet is sounding over the earth, and God is coming suddenly to His temple!

A New Anointing

In this great move of the Spirit of God, we are seeing the vast unfolding of God's prophetic mantle over all the earth upon His servants. God is raising up prophets—men and women in whom he has placed His vision, along with a deep spirit of intercession and warfare and a supernatural sensitivity to hear His voice. Lookouts who keep watch day and night are posted high up on the Church's walls.

When I speak of the prophetic mantle, I am referring to the anointing and the authority with which the Holy Spirit dresses selected people in the Church to reveal and manifest Christ, His profoundness and His knowledge under the perfect order of divine structure. This anointing enables God's prophets to hear clearly His voice, revealing to us His marvelous and hidden mysteries. As it is written in the book of Isaiah, "I will give you the treasures of darkness, riches stored in secret places, so that you may know that I am the Lord, the God of Israel, who summons you by name" (Isa. 45:3). Scripture also says, "God has revealed it to us by his Spirit. The Spirit searches all things, even the deep things of God" (1 Cor. 2:10).

Christ is coming soon, and it is necessary that His beloved be ready, raised up knowing the voice of her Husband. The Church that is awake praises Him and says, "Listen! My lover! Look! Here he comes" (Song of Songs 2:8).

This is the time when God wants to speak to His people to prepare the time of His coming, just as the prophetic mantle came upon John the Baptist to prepare the way for Christ:

> A voice of one calling: "In the desert prepare the way for the LORD; make straight in the wilderness a highway for our God. Every valley shall be raised up, every mountain and hill made low; the rough ground shall become level, the rugged places a plain. And the glory of the LORD will be revealed, and all mankind together will see it" (Isa. 40:3-5).

Likewise, God is unfolding an anointing that will raise up men and women of God, and many will listen. His voice will be like a double-edged sword, penetrating to divide soul and spirit, joints and marrow. His voice will be heard in the middle of the desert, the place of desolation and defeat where millions of believers are currently living. The voice of His prophets will be heard in such a way and come in such power on God's part that it will tear down every spiritual arrogance, raising up the downcast and strengthening the weak-kneed and humble in heart.

In Response, an Army!

This mighty voice of God's prophets will raise up the glorious army of God in all power and majesty, the army that the prophet Joel saw:

> Blow the trumpet in Zion; sound the alarm on my holy hill. Let all who live in the land tremble, for the day of the LORD is coming. It is close at hand—a day of darkness and gloom, a day of clouds and blackness. Like dawn spreading across the mountains a large and mighty army comes,

> such as never was of old nor ever will be in ages to come. Before them fire devours, behind them a flame blazes. Before them the land is like the garden of Eden, behind them, a desert waste—nothing escapes them. They have the appearance of horses; they gallop along like cavalry. With a noise like that of chariots they leap over the mountain-tops, like a crackling fire consuming stubble, like a mighty army drawn up for battle. At the sight of them, nations are in anguish; every face turns pale. They charge like warriors; they scale walls like soldiers. They all march in line, not swerving from their course. They do not jostle each other; each marches straight ahead. They plunge through defenses without breaking ranks. They rush upon the city; they run along the wall. They climb into the houses; like thieves they enter through the windows. Before them the earth shakes, the sky trembles, the sun and moon are darkened, and the stars no longer shine. The LORD thunders at the head of his army; his forces are beyond number, and mighty are those who obey his command. The day of the LORD is great; it is dreadful. Who can endure it? (Joel 2:1-11).

God's Spirit is announcing a time in which we are going to see an army of prayer, intercession and spiritual warriors raised up, the likes of which has never been seen before. A Church with tiny prayer groups is not going to shake the nations. But God is raising up an army empowered with the fire, might and authority of the living God—an army that will challenge the gates of hell.

His is an army born in the midst of divine visitation, whose mouths are lighted coals and before whose cry God descends from His holy dwelling place.

It is an army sustained and dressed in the right hand of His power, one that causes the gust of God's breath to strip the foundations of the earth and leave them exposed to the rebuke of the Almighty.

It is an army whose prayer is so full of the pain and anguish of God for man's condition that it shakes the powers of the heavens and makes the earth tremble.

Arrayed in David's Mantle

This army wears the same prophetic mantle that came upon David through the hand of the prophet Samuel. Hannah, the prophet's mother, had poured out her soul during a time in which the people of Israel were dying from spiritual hunger and desolation (see 1 Sam. 1:10,11). The nation and the priesthood had degenerated through the carelessness of the high priest Eli, and the Temple had been desecrated by his sons (see 1 Sam. 2:12,17). God needed a soul to cry out, a soul who would stand in the gap for the restoration of divine principles.

God heard Hannah's cry, and in her womb He formed an awakening of a new generation of prophets that would bring the order of God to His people and take the nation to its greatest splendor of glory: the reign of Solomon. Hannah's cry resulted in the prophetic mantle being bestowed on her son Samuel, who later would confer it upon David.

David, the man after God's own heart, was full of

- the faith of God,
- the knowledge of the heart of God,
- a spirit of worship,
- a prophetic anointing,

- a heartfelt cry in prayer,
- the anointing of warfare.

David changed history by subduing all his enemies and receiving from God the blueprint for bringing the glory of God into His holy Temple.

We hear about how many people are crying to God for a great revival in these days; but revival certainly will not come before God raises up a prophetic move of intercession, divine direction and warfare that brings to light the pits of iniquity that have become strongholds over our cities and nations.

I believe there are cities and regions that cannot be penetrated with the gospel until a determined action conquers the forces of darkness which hold them captive. David understood this need. He knew that the only way to confront the forces of evil was to reach the heart of God—prostrate, groaning for victory—and to worship God for His greatness:

> In my distress I called to the LORD; I cried to my God for help. From his temple he heard my voice; my cry came before him, into his ears. The earth trembled and quaked, and the foundations of the mountains shook; they trembled because he was angry (Ps. 18:6,7).

God is shaping hearts to be like that of David's heart. He wants hearts that do not cry out of vain religiosity but beat in sync with the Lord's own heart; hearts that are able to hear His weeping and feel as He feels; hearts that perceive His holy indignation over this lost world and, at the same time, are touched with the depth of His love for His creation and His children.

We know God's heart. Although His people are determined to turn from Him, yet He leads "them with cords of human kindness, with ties of love"; He lifts "the yoke from their neck and ben[ds] down to feed them" (Hos. 11:4-7). He continues to speak through Hosea in infinite mercy from the depths of His heart: "How can I give you up? . . . How can I hand you over? . . . My heart is changed within me; all my compassion is aroused" (Hos. 11:8).

David cried with God, shaken and moved by the love of God, until the heavens and earth trembled, until justice came, until the delivering hand of his powerful God overcame his enemies. David did not settle for simple, structured prayers. He yearned passionately for God's presence, pouring himself out in worship even at the cost of being humbled. His prayer was so powerful that the Scripture says of God:

> Smoke rose from his nostrils; consuming fire came from his mouth, burning coals blazed out of it. He parted the heavens and came down; dark clouds were under his feet. The LORD thundered from heaven; the voice of the Most High resounded. He shot his arrows and scattered the enemies, great bolts of lightning and routed them (Ps. 18:8,9,13,14).

The prophetic anointing on David caused the heavens to bow down and the presence of God to come forth, bringing a visitation of such magnitude that the enemy was unable to face it. God spoke and judgment came; the fire of God descended and consumed. At the same time, the revelation of a new and glorious tabernacle was presented to David in a vision of angelic worship before the throne of God.

This same anointing is being poured out by the Holy Spirit today. It is an anointing born in the heart of God and coming from His throne. This prophetic mantle will bring about an even greater visitation of the Holy Spirit, enabling many to understand the secrets of God and tearing down even the most difficult strongholds, principalities and powers of darkness.

This is the time when the weak will be raised up, and the downcast and afflicted in spirit will become the valiant in God's army. This is the time when small shepherds in the fields will be transformed into kings who will govern the nations with an iron rod. It is a time when even the smallest will be raised up, and the vile and scorned will be called the greatest in the Lord's house.

The prophetic anointing comes, as in the case of the prophet Jeremiah and the prophet Daniel, as a manifestation of deep intercessory prayer that identifies with the sin of the people. It cries out in lamentation for the Church's condition and declares at the same time the judgment that God is going to bring about.

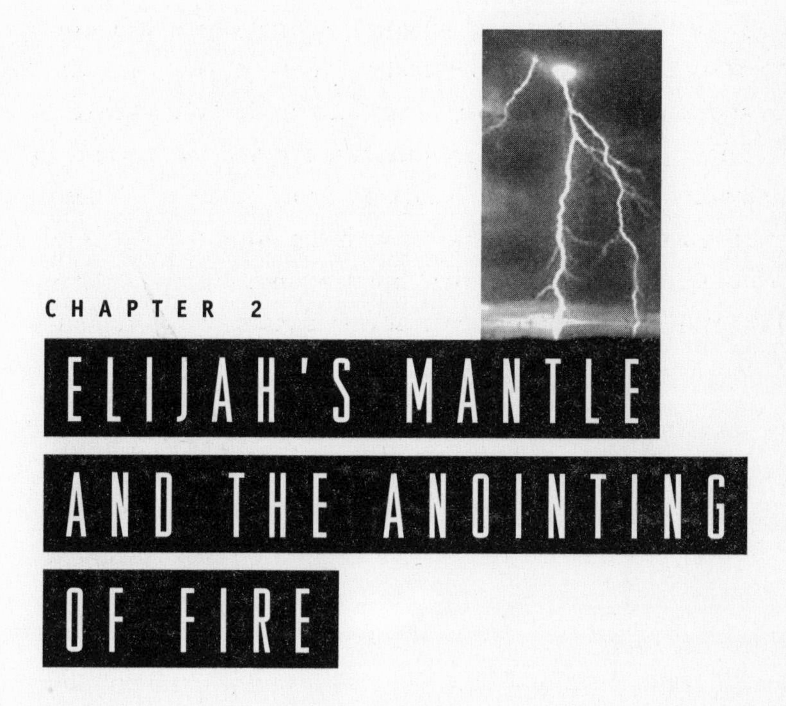

CHAPTER 2

ELIJAH'S MANTLE AND THE ANOINTING OF FIRE

The prophetic anointing in our times is descending like the divine manifestation of the Holy Spirit upon the prophet Elijah of old. This move of the Spirit was foretold by the apostle Peter, after he revealed that the risen Christ would return at the "restoration" in the last days through the fulfillment of prophecy:

> For Moses said, "The Lord your God will raise up for you a prophet like me from among your own people; you

must listen to everything he tells you. Anyone who does not listen to him will be completely cut off from among his people.

"Indeed, all the prophets from Samuel on, as many as have spoken, have foretold these days. And you are heirs of the prophets and of the covenant God made with your fathers. He said to Abraham, 'Through your offspring all peoples on earth will be blessed'" (Acts 3:22-25).

Here the Spirit is prophesying that when the time of restoration of all things comes, a prophetic spirit will be poured out like never before in history. It will be the life-giving voice of Jesus Christ speaking through the Holy Spirit and bringing about the fulfillment of everything that has been spoken since ancient times. It will be the trumpet of God that enlists His chosen army. It will be the voice of God awakening the Spirit of prophecy that is described by the angel in Revelation: "For the substance (essence) of the truth revealed by Jesus is the spirit of all prophecy [the vital breath, the inspiration of all inspired preaching and interpretation of the divine will and purpose]" (Rev. 19:10, *AMP*).

This manifestation of the Holy Spirit will give content and meaning to God's covenant with His children, making them rulers over the godless, lights in the midst of darkness, torches of fire that kindle other fires. It will be the divine anointing that raises up God's people to be the blessing for all the peoples of the earth.

This is the same manifestation of the Spirit of God that came upon Elijah, of which the Lord Jesus Christ prophesied:

"To be sure, Elijah comes and will restore all things. But I tell you, Elijah has already come, and they did not rec-

> ognize him, but have done to him everything they wished. In the same way the Son of Man is going to suffer at their hands." Then the disciples understood that he was talking to them about John the Baptist (Matt. 17:11-13).

This appearance of God's Spirit, whom He sends for specific purposes at determinant moments of history, is preparing the earth for the second coming of Christ just as it did for His first coming. The prophet Malachi prophesied of this momentous occasion:

> For behold, the day comes that shall burn like an oven, and all the proud and arrogant, yes, and all that do wickedly and are lawless, shall be stubble; the day that comes shall burn them up, says the Lord of hosts, so that it will leave them neither root nor branch. But unto you who revere and worshipfully fear My name shall the Sun of Righteousness arise with healing in His wings and His beams, and you shall go forth and gambol like calves [released] from the stall and leap for joy. And you shall tread down the lawless and wicked, for they shall be ashes under the soles of your feet in the day that I shall do this, says the Lord of hosts. Behold, I will send you Elijah the prophet before the great and terrible day of the Lord comes. And he shall turn and reconcile the hearts of the [estranged] fathers to the [ungodly] children, and the hearts of the [rebellious] children to [the piety of] their fathers [a reconciliation produced by repentance of the ungodly;] lest I come and smite the land with a curse and a ban of utter destruction (Mal. 4:1-3,5,6, *AMP*).

The Call to Holy Living

The prophetic mantle that was upon Elijah and later came upon John the Baptist will bring with it the presence of God's Spirit to convict the world of sin, righteousness and judgment (see John 16:8-11), scrutinizing it in a way that has not been known since the beginning of the world. It is essential that every Christian understand the vast importance of living under this scrutiny in holiness, without which, the Word declares, nobody will see the Lord (see Heb. 12:14). God is speaking and producing through the Holy Spirit an overflowing fruit of repentance and understanding of the important position a holy Church has in preparing the way of the Lord. We see this reflected in the ministry of John the Baptist:

> John said to the crowds coming out to be baptized by him, "You brood of vipers! Who warned you to flee from the coming wrath? Produce fruit in keeping with repentance. And do not begin to say to yourselves, 'We have Abraham as our father.' For I tell you that out of these stones God can raise up children for Abraham. The ax is already at the root of the trees, and every tree that does not produce good fruit will be cut down and thrown into the fire" (Luke 3:7-9).

Unfortunately, despite such warnings, the Church today in its laziness, God's people in their lukewarmness and complacency, is saying "We can continue walking at ease, flirting with the world, because God is a God of mercy and because He has placed pastors among us to do the work."

Thus, for God to bring about the greatest manifestation of His glory He has to bring a revival of repentance over the Church.

When we talk about spiritual warfare and the war that has already been declared by God, we must understand that the first battle to be faced is against the strongholds of sin and indolence in our own lives. It is a war of faith, hope against hope, that will bring us to our knees before the Cross, crucifying our fleshly and sinful desires.

But the power to accomplish this death to sin and resurrection to holiness has been unleashed! The Spirit of the all-powerful living God dwells within you and is upon you to undo the works of the devil. Thus says the Spirit:

> *There is no power, no stronghold, no demonic attack that the Spirit of God living in you cannot destroy. Any other argument is deceitful, and comes from Satan, the father of lies. For the weapons of our warfare are not carnal, but mighty in God to demolish strongholds, taking captive every thought, every argument, every pretension, to make us obedient to Christ.*

Before revival, before the great harvest of the last days comes, there has to be a move of repentance and intercession so powerful that we see an army of God's people blessed with the anointing and the authority of God to snatch away souls from the devil with a holy and spiritual violence.

During the preaching of Charles Finney, the man of God who was used in one of the greatest revivals of his time, the fire of the Holy Spirit came, convicting people of sin so mightily that people literally felt the flames of hell and multitudes fell prostrate at the feet of Christ. This did not happen because of the courage of a great preacher but because Charles Finney knew that the Lord of hosts "is a man of war" (Exod. 15:3, *KJV*).

Finney conquered nations for Christ, because he withdrew to the woods and in the quietness of nature began to weep and intercede for those who were imprisoned by Satan. He yearned for souls in such a way that his whole being was clothed in the Holy Spirit. He groaned with such deep pain that the foundations of the heavens shook, and God came down with His angels and began to break the chains of those held captive and to remove the scales of spiritual blindness from their eyes.

The prophetic mantle that is being unfolded as the manifestation of Elijah's spirit is the voice from heaven that is saying:

Every spirit that cannot be transformed, every ministry that cannot be changed by the power of my Spirit is dead. The axe is already at the roots, and they will be cut off.

The Baptism of Fire

One day the Lord showed me His heart and allowed me to touch His tears. His voice spoke to me, saying:

Cry, cry for my people, because many of those whose faces you have seen will be cut off. I have interceded for them, but they do not want to listen to the voice of My Spirit. I am going to send a fire that will raise up My army, it will raise up My glorious Church, in whom I am going to show great signs that eye has never seen or ear ever heard; but this fire is going to consume the rebellious!

My whole being agonized with divine sorrow, a grief like Jesus felt in the garden of Gethsemane when He poured out his soul: "My soul is overwhelmed with sorrow to the point of death" (Matt. 26:38). He was already seeing those who would reject His blood, those who would never produce fruit, those who having known the Word would return to worldly ways, those who would be cut off from the olive branch; and He was crying and coming undone with love for them.

John the Baptist promised two ingredients that would give the Church the power to overcome the world: the Holy Spirit and a divine fire. John said, "I baptize you with water. But one more powerful than I will come, the thongs of whose sandals I am not worthy to untie. He will baptize you with the Holy Spirit and with fire" (Luke 3:16).

The word "baptize" means to submerge, to immerse, to dye (as cloth is plunged into colored water to change its hue). The baptism of the Holy Spirit and fire is descending upon the Church, bringing with it a conviction to men's hearts so strong that they fall prostrate before God in repentance, saying "What should I do Lord? Here am I!"

The Spirit of the Lord has been sent to prepare the second coming of Christ through a glorious visitation of divine fire that will convert and clean the souls of God's people and straighten the way before Him. Hear the voice of the Spirit sounding the trumpet to recruit you:

> *Gird up your loins of understanding and get ready for God's battle. All those who do not hear, who have become deafened by the noise of sin, by the pride and filth of this world, will be cut off. The axe is already in place.*

Listen again to the prophet Malachi:

> "See, I will send my messenger, who will prepare the way before me. Then suddenly the Lord you are seeking will come to his temple; the messenger of the covenant,

> whom you desire, will come," says the LORD Almighty. But who can endure the day of his coming? Who can stand when he appears? For he will be like a refiner's fire or a launderer's soap. He will sit as a refiner and purifier of silver; he will purify the Levites and refine them like gold and silver. Then the LORD will have men who will bring offerings in righteousness (Mal. 3:1-3).

Our God and His Holy Spirit are like a refining fire!

Much of what has been preached about the baptism of fire has been about trials in general. However, I see many people who go through trial after trial without ever experiencing God's fire. There is an important distinction to make among trials:

1. Those that come as a consequence of sin
2. Those sent directly from heaven for our growth
3. Those that lead us to a meeting with the divine fire

Unfortunately, the majority of trials that Christians undergo are of the first type—those that are the result of our transgressions and disobedience, those that come because there are open doors in our lives through which the devil can enter to steal, kill and destroy. Trials of this kind are reprimands from the heavenly Father, and they can never bring His fire.

The second type of trial consists of the Lord's instructions in His inscrutable ways, leading us to maturity.

It is the third kind of trial in which the hand of the Almighty takes us and introduces us to the valley of the shadow of death, where His rod and staff give comfort. It is the third group of trials that causes the glorious Spirit of God to rest upon us. As the apostle Peter wrote:

> Dear friends, do not be surprised at the painful trial you are suffering, as though something strange were happening to you. But rejoice that you participate in the sufferings of Christ, so that you may be overjoyed when his glory is revealed (1 Pet. 4:12,13).

Such trials are places of breaking where you pass the boundaries of the natural to meet face-to-face with God. It is the rugged climb of our personal Sinai to enter into God's fire. It is when, at the end of the valley, you hear the voice of the Spirit saying "I anoint your head with oil—your cup overflows." It is the sublime moment after the burnt offering when the smell of fat rises as a fragrant aroma into the Most Holy Place.

This kind of fire is something very deep. It is the manifestation of irresistible power. This kind of fire is of divine origin. It is a glorious manifestation of God's presence that burns away the scum from our lives, refining us into vessels of silver and gold. It is the rain of heavenly fire that falls to earth to consume us with repentance and to clothe the spirit of man with power to climb to the summit of the mount where God Himself dwells. This fire is God's glory like that which was seen on the day of the miraculous catch of fish, when Peter fell prostrate and said, "Go away from me, Lord; I am a sinful man!" (Luke 5:8).

This fire is the very *Shekinah* of God, the Almighty's glory manifested, the radiant fire that we cannot face without taking off our shoes, falling on our faces and saying "Father, this is holy ground, because Your presence is filling it."

It is the same fire that shone in the burning bush that attracted Moses' attention in the wilderness. There was no trial, and there was no shame for Moses; the fire was the glorious manifestation that was going to raise him up as Israel's deliverer, the revelation of the living God that would take him before

Pharaoh. It was the strength, the *dunamis* of God the all powerful with which Moses would confront the empire of darkness. It was the fullness of the Spirit in its plenitude that would enable him to stand before the proud and feared Egyptian empire and say, "Pharaoh, thus says the Lord, . . . *Let My people go*" (Exod. 5:1, *AMP*, emphasis added).

The Militant and Authoritative Word

This same fire is descending today upon the Church, raising up men and women anointed with the authority of God to stand before the devil. They will become true warriors in prayer, soldiers in God's army capable of releasing God's authoritative Word, storming the gates of hell and ordering the powers and principalities, saying "In the Name of Jesus, let God's people go!"

The anointing, the prophetic mantle is touching lips with fire, with burning coals, creating throats that loose their voices as arrows, that come forth as the anointed arrow of Elisha decreeing, "The Lord's arrow of victory, the arrow of victory over Aram!" (2 Kings 13:17)

It is the voice ignited by the same flame of prophetic fire that will shake our nations, tearing down the strongholds of evil and devastating the devil's kingdom. It is the word decreed by the apostle Paul "in order that the manifold wisdom of God might now be made known through the church to the rulers and the authorities in the heavenly places" (Eph. 3:10, *NASB*).

How much the Church needs men and women clothed with the authority of God's prophetic word! Too often we do not see this authority because the majority seek methods that have already been used to cast out demons. It seems easier to ask how someone else confronted the principalities and powers than to humble and deny ourselves until we meet face-to-face with the fire and hear God's voice resounding in our own spirit.

It is then that you know that you know God is with you. It is then that you are able to stand in front of the oppressor of your nation, the torturer of your city and he who causes anguish to your family, and say with total certainty in the power of God's Spirit, "Satan, as the Lord Almighty before whom I stand lives, *in the name of Jesus, COME OUT!*"

It is the name of Jesus Christ, united with the anointed word, that will unleash a power so great that the foundations of the devil's kingdom will tremble, and neither powers nor principalities nor the rulers of darkness will be able to resist it.

The devil knows who Jesus is, he knows who Paul is, and he knows who God's anointed ones are—those who are faithful to bear His authoritative Word.

The anointing of fire is coming down as the prophetic mantle that was upon Elijah. It is an anointing of spiritual violence: "From the days of John the Baptist until now the kingdom of heaven suffers violence, and violent men take it by force" (Matt. 11:12, *NASB*).

It is a military anointing to confront the forces of the devil, to shake the weak thoughts of those who falter between God's love and the love of this world, which is enmity to God. It is an aggressive, warlike anointing that takes hold of the promises of God, filling us with the revelation and the knowledge of who we are as the children of the Omnipotent:

> I pray that the eyes of your heart may be enlightened, so that you may know what is the hope of His calling, what are the riches of the glory of His inheritance in the saints, and what is the surpassing greatness of His power

> toward us who believe. . . . which He brought about in Christ, when He raised Him from the dead (Eph. 1:18-20, *NASB*).

A Time of Rescue and Restoration

A manifestation of the power of God is coming in our days that will set apart and sanctify the Church. It is a time of rescuing all that can be rescued and restoring all that can be restored.

God is sending an anointing of inner strength, an anointing that reveals the living and effective weapons of our warfare, because God is showing the world the power of His true Church.

> "In that day," declares the LORD, "I will gather the lame; I will assemble the exiles and those I have brought to grief. I will make the lame a remnant, those driven away a strong nation. The LORD will rule over them in Mount Zion from that day and forever. As for you, O watchtower of the flock, O stronghold of the Daughter of Zion, the former dominion will be restored to you; kingship will come to the Daughter of Jerusalem. Rise and thresh, O Daughter of Zion, for I will give you horns of iron; I will give you hoofs of bronze and you will break to pieces many nations." You will devote their ill-gotten gains to the LORD, their wealth to the Lord of all the earth (Micah 4:6-8,13).

The trumpet is being sounded. Rejoice, O daughter of Zion, because your time of desolation has ended! God is causing rain in the desert!

The fire has to be poured out to make straight the way of the Lord. Before Satan's attack on the Church, the Lord comes as a purifying fire to burn all the dross from those who are His. The foundations are being shaken so every disciple can clearly see that he is founded on the rock, which is Christ:

> For no one can lay any foundation other than the one already laid, which is Jesus Christ. If any man builds on this foundation using gold, silver, costly stones, wood, hay or straw, his work will be shown for what it is, because the Day will bring it to light. It will be revealed with fire, and the fire will test the quality of each man's work (1 Cor. 3:11-13).

When will this day be that will bring all things to light? Romans 13:12 says: "The night is nearly over; the day is almost here. So let us put aside the deeds of darkness and put on the armor of light."

War has been declared, and we have already been given the weapons to destroy the devil's empire. The fire comes to burn up that which is of no use and to dress us in the invincibility of Jesus Christ. The prophetic mantle in the anointing of Elijah is a divine power that opens spiritual eyes to see into the secret chambers of the devil, to see the strategies of the enemy before they are launched and to undo his plans in his own quarters.

The stronghold of the devil can be stormed by surprise; the walls of his kingdom are breachable, because Satan has been destroyed, his empire exposed to rebuke and crushed on the cross by the blood of Him who ascended to the throne; the King of kings and Lord of lords, before whom every knee must bow. Glory to Christ, who lives and reigns forever!

A Spirit of Prayer and Revelation

The spirit of Elijah is also the one bold enough to stand before the devil's forces and to reveal the truth: "As the LORD, the God of Israel, lives, whom I serve, there will be neither dew nor rain in the next few years except at my word" (1 Kings 17:1). It decrees judgment upon Satan's kingdom and brings destruction on the enemy's ground.

It is also a deep spirit of prayer which enters heavenly dimensions; it is a spirit of divine wisdom, of supernatural direction from God. It is a spirit that submerges us in God's presence, bringing us to a place of dependence upon the move of the Omnipotent, like the cherubim in Ezekiel's vision who moved in unison with the glory of God.

Those who are born of the Spirit are like the wind that blows wherever it pleases and you can hear its sound, but you cannot tell from where it comes or where it is going (see John 3:8). This Spirit reveals the mysteries of Christ, carrying us along by the wind, a gentle whisper like that which spoke to Elijah the prophet to anoint kings and prophets, and enabling us to see the 7,000 who had not bowed their knees to Baal.

It is a manifestation of the Spirit that lifts up our prayer and lets it ascend before the ark of glory in the heavenly tabernacle. It is a prayer like the one the apostle John describes in the vision of the revelation that comes forth from the golden altar before God (see Rev. 8). We stand at the place where the angel came down and offered incense with the prayers of the saints, and the smoke of the incense went up before God from the angel's hand. These prayers are bold, as when the angel took the censer, filled it with fire from the altar and hurled it on the earth; and there came peals of thunder, rumblings, flashes of lightning and an earthquake. God is raising up warriors and intercessors who literally produce earthquakes in the heavens and the earth.

The Spirit is producing expectant prayer, the kind of prayer that knows something is going to happen because it is backed up by the word of faith, which is the substance, the certainty and conviction of that which cannot be seen. Prayer that comes from those who by the Spirit can look at things that cannot be seen and know that they will pass from the invisible to the visible realm. It was in the midst of drought that Elijah saw the rain which was lashing the heavens in the invisible realm of the Spirit. He loosed the word, believing with conviction that God would back it up. After his servant shouted, "A cloud as small as a man's hand is rising from the sea," the prophet ran to Ahab the king and told him, "Hitch up your chariot and go down before the rain stops you" (1 Kings 18:44).

Likewise, God is speaking to the Church and telling her:

The move of My Spirit you have seen up until now has been only the size of a palm of the hand. But a rain is about to come upon My people which will shake the powers of the heavens and the earth with the power of My right hand.

The time has come for God to reveal Himself, and the pagan gods and those who serve them will be ashamed. It is the hour of which those who are arrayed in the power of God will say, like Elijah:

- The God who answers with fire, He is God!
- The God who baptizes us with fire, He is God!
- The God who changes men's hearts, He is God!
- The God who disperses our enemies, He is God!
- The God who heals the hopeless and raises the dead, He is God!

Awake! Shine and Be Radiant!

For too long the Church has been lethargic and idle, allowing Satan to gain ground that was bought and given to us by the price of the blood of Christ.

The time has come to wake up. The time has come to stop the devil's work and to tear down the gates of hell.

Satan has been confident through the ages because he has faced only a fearful Christianity, and he has become accustomed to finding little resistance to his attacks. As a result, he has not learned how to defend himself, because he has never been attacked until these times when God is organizing an army with His wisdom and power. Today God commands His people:

> Arise [from the depression and prostration in which circumstances have kept you—rise to a new life]! Shine (be radiant with the glory of the Lord), for your light has come, and the glory of the Lord has risen upon you! (Isa. 60:1, *AMP*).

This is the time for God's prophets to loose the Word and for the fire to be poured down. This is the moment in which the double portion will be released, because the glory of the latter house will be greater than that of the former. This is the day that will bring deliverance to the captives, the opening of prison doors to those who are bound, healing to the sick and the oil of joy to those who are mourning.

For too long the Church has allowed spirits of division, criticism, judgment, envy, sectarianism and jealousy. God has said, "Enough! My Church is like the valley of dry bones that I showed to my prophet Ezekiel":

> Then he said to me, "Prophesy to these bones and say to them, 'Dry bones, hear the word of the LORD! This is what the Sovereign LORD says to these bones: I will make breath enter you, and you will come to life. I will attach tendons to you and make flesh come upon you and cover you with skin; I will put breath in you, and you will come to life. Then you will know that I am the LORD'" (Ezek. 37:4-6).

It is necessary that the same God intervene now, so we can see real unity in the Church. And this is one of the reasons He is making his prophetic mantle descend.

The prophets of God are those who are full of the anointing and will be able to prophesy and see how the Spirit begins to join bone to bone. This will not be the work of any man but the work of God's Holy Spirit. Even in the midst of prevailing division, we have started to see bones come alive and come together. But we will never know the potential, never see the Body's tendons at work and the flesh cover its bones (that is to say, the essence and revelation of Christ in His infinite depth) until all the bones are joined.

It is necessary that men and women chosen, refined and extremely sensitive to the voice of God be raised up, knowing the times and the Lord's will, prophesying to the Spirit: "Come from the four winds, O breath, and breathe into these slain, that they may live" (Ezek. 37:9).

And as Ezekiel saw it happen, we will see the Church revived, rising firmly to its feet to form a tremendous army. It is a fundamental necessity to receive this revelation in order for God to make all our enemies a footstool for Christ—enemies whom God has already given into our hands but over whom God has left to us the great responsibility of establishing this victory unto the ends of the earth for His glory and honor.

God is already doing it. All over the world His army is receiving the anointing from heaven and taking up His mandate to declare war without precedent on the devil.

It is a time of war. And it is a time of victory!

CHAPTER 3

MY PILGRIMAGE FROM DARKNESS TO LIGHT

Although I feel it necessary to share briefly part of my personal testimony, I will not go into detail, because doing so has caused some to focus on the darkness in which I was enveloped instead of the light into which I was delivered. The terrible and frightening years of my past seem very remote and far from me today, but I cannot deny them; and how my soul trembles not only with their remembrance but also because of God's infinite love in bringing me through them. As dark as those days were, if I had not lived through those dark days of horror and surrender to demonic forces, I would not be able to appreciate the light as I do; nor would I have the clear perspective and knowledge about the kingdom of darkness to use in spiritual warfare.

The web that entangles so many in Satan's service seems so indestructible that it may seem that no one can come out alive to God. But nothing is impossible for the Lion of Judah, for the King of kings and Lord of lords. Jesus Christ, who penetrated the inner parts of that other world, called me by name and, taking me by the hand, brought me into the Kingdom of His glorious light so that today I can unveil the secrets of our enemy's kingdom for His glory.

Set Apart for Service

In spite of the awful deceit with which Satan had entangled me, I never stopped searching for God. The Lord knew it would be this way, and He set me apart for His service from the foundations of the world. When I was only 18, Jesus came down from the highest place to visit me in a totally supernatural and unexplainably beautiful way to safeguard me from the terrible abominations I would commit and from pacts with Satan I would make that would have otherwise taken my soul to the gates of death.

It was night, and the sky was cloudy due to the rainy season. I was in my room preparing for a final exam when something distracted me from my studies. I began to feel the impulse that some powerful force like a magnet was drawing me irresistibly toward the window. It was much stronger than I, and I could not ignore its beckoning. So I got up in great curiosity to see what was on the other side of the windowpane.

To my surprise, when I looked up at the sky, which was covered with dense clouds, I saw a marvelous light shining like a giant star that nothing could darken. For several moments I tried unsuccessfully to come up with an explanation for the incredible beauty I was beholding. Then a wonder happened. A more intense beam of light came out of the star and entered my room, filling it completely with a dazzling brightness.

I fell as if dead to the floor. I could not lift up my face; I was totally paralyzed, unable to make the slightest movement. Uncontrollable tears began to flow from my eyes, coming forth from the depth of my unbelieving heart before the reality that such infinite kindness and incredible love, impossible to define with human words, really existed.

The mixed feelings I felt within me clashed with each other. On the one hand I felt like the smallest and most unclean person on Earth, but on the other I felt that I was the most fortunate of all women. My eyes saw what they saw and my ears heard what they heard, but my mind was incapable of understanding this, which was beyond all comprehension.

Suddenly I stopped looking at the incredible light that was surrounding me. It was as the ecstasy the apostle Paul describes—I did not know whether I was in the body or out of the body, in my room or caught up into the "third heaven" (2 Cor. 12:2). I do know that in that place where time does not exist, my eyes saw the greatness of God's throne. Above all, I realized that I was immersed in absolute wisdom, where all knowledge coexists in perfect harmony. While I was there, I seemed to know everything, and nothing could hide itself from me.

How much time passed, I do not know; but when the vision left and little by little my room returned into view again, I found a paper written in a trembling hand—my hand, during that experience—that recorded the message Christ wanted me to remember:

I am Jesus Christ your Lord, and I have come to tell you that in His time I will make Myself known to you, because you are My servant. I will come to you through a man with blue eyes.

Fading Vision, Dying Fire

That visitation marked my youth. I did not know what to do. Nobody had ever spoken to me about Jesus being a personal Savior. Even less did I know about the existence of a Christian church where they read the Bible. The only Christianity I knew was a kind of Catholicism that is common in Latin America—a mixture of ancient pagan religions and the Christian faith. Because that was all I knew, I started attending Mass every day, believing that this would bring me nearer to Jesus.

Within a short time, I moved to France and lived in the city of Paris for almost two years. In this cold country so far from God, my faith dried up. Little by little I became discouraged. That marvelous fire went out.

The day arrived when I no longer felt that my beloved Jesus was present in the Mass. Only God knows how much and with what desperation I searched until, disillusioned, I stopped attending Mass.

It was during this lapse of seeking and subsequent frustration that the devil did not miss the opportunity to trap me. I started to become involved in all that sounded spiritual to me. The world uses what it defines as spiritual to promote experiences that raise man's spirit to levels it believes to be closer to its creator. In my ignorance and thirst to find something that beckoned to me but eluded me, my mind and conscience accepted any kind of spiritualism as something good. It was this undiscerning quest that eventually led me to experiment with Haitian Voodooism.

What I did not know was that I was entering through invisible gates into the spiritual territory governed by the prince of darkness: an existential realm as real as the one our eyes see and our senses touch but one that is foreign to the Spirit of God. We must understand that just as God is spirit, so are the devil and his hosts; and they in turn can appeal to the spirit of man.

In our everyday world there is a legal principle which affirms that "ignorance of the law is no excuse." Unfortunately, ignorance of the spiritual dimension and the laws which rule it makes us fall into grave errors that can lead to eternal destruction. As the proverb says, "There is a way that seems right to a man, but in the end it leads to death" (Prov. 14:12). And as God said through the prophet, "My people are destroyed from lack of knowledge" (Hos. 4:6).

We do not have to cast more than a glance around us to see thousands of people suffering needlessly, in great pain because of their own ignorance, committing themselves to open all kinds of doors without realizing that they are opening themselves to the devil. "I didn't know" is their excuse, because they have not been taught; yet it is their own fault, because they have not felt the duty of every human being to seek the truth (see 2 Thess. 2:9-11).

Yet Jesus respected my free will and did not intervene in my downhill slide into magic, in my search of the supernatural, which left me finding the false power of the prince of darkness. Longing for a message from the world beyond, I began to dabble in the use of Ouija boards and the supposed truths of automatic writing. I tried so-called white magic—although it has actually never existed but is only another form of black magic. I sank into the practices of Voodoo, the dark side of idolatry, and a long list of esoteric practices and abominable deceptions.

Through it all, however, Jesus never stopped protecting me; He never abandoned me in the most dangerous situations; He never left my side.

Why? So His eternal purpose would be fulfilled in my life: to denounce all over the world the falseness and terrible consequences that hide behind the apparently innocent games of occultism; to come to understand the secrets behind the practices of these false paths of spirituality; and to warn others that they culminate in the very gates of hell.

In other words, God was allowing the groundwork for a powerful ministry of spiritual warfare and deliverance to be forged in me. And if I say it is powerful, it is not boasting in human ability but in the power of Him whom I have believed and who works within me: Christ in us, the hope of glory! In allowing me to discover Satan in the depths of darkness, He would lead me first to expose the devil and then to announce the virtues of Him who brings us out of darkness to the light.

In history, the greatest strategies of war have been accomplished by those who knew the most about their adversaries. I thank God for His mercy toward me, for choosing the foolish things of this world to shame the wise and for proving that where sin abounds, grace abounds more. I thank Him that out of my miserable experiences has come a ministry of deliverance to numerous others who were oppressed by the devil.

God's specialty is to take the worst of your existence and to convert it into the best, using it for His glory. To Him be all the honor, all the glory, all the power!

Battling the Demonic

Before I was ready and able to use my experiences for God's glory, the enemy caused me to experience tremendous torture and psychic pain. Physical pain cannot be compared to the pain of the soul. My being was home to incredible demonic spirits who beat me at their fancy, destroying my life, my family and all that I had.

Day and night, year after year, their torment harassed me without any rest. They looked meticulously for ways to control my life. They tore my soul apart time and time again. They fought within me, taking me to the point of suicide and self-destruction. On numerous occasions I looked for comfort and answers from a psychiatrist who did not know how to respond to me. I went from one to another, but none of them knew how to help me. Finally, I wound up in a psychiatric hospital.

I spent entire nights in vigil, with the devil and his hosts visiting me in visible form. Sometimes they came to give me orders; other times they came for the pleasure of seeing me suffer, filling my routine with the torture of feeling that I had to pay for past favors. But no matter how much I paid, the debt never decreased but only grew greater. It was as though a chain was being wrapped around me, with more force at each attack, to ensure that I would never escape Satan's sentence of death. At times when his demons came to torture me, I was left in bed with a deep depression for days.

I came to understand how the soul anesthetizes itself when it reaches the point of breaking, of being torn apart inwardly. I use the phrase "torn apart" because I could feel their claws that were tearing me to shreds within. Then a kind of lethargy would set in and I could not feel anything for a while, until the pain returned—each time stronger than the last.

The devil took me to the deepest chambers of hell where I saw lost souls being beaten and burnt to the destructive joy of their executioners. On one occasion I entered through one of the tunnels of death and saw thousands of skeletonlike beings outrageously dressed. With distorted faces full of desperation and helplessness, they tried to keep me in that dark place.

I know very well what the Bible means when it uses the phrase "utter darkness" (Isa. 8:22). It is when life appears to have no ray of hope, when there is no escape from anguish, loneliness and sorrow.

I know what it is to have spent almost a year with the face of death pursuing me day and night, watching over my bed, getting into the car with me, listening to every conversation, with the words of an insane litany not ceasing to echo within me: *I'm coming for you, I'm coming for you, I'm coming for you.*

Perhaps I can dare to say I am one of those who have been able to feel just a part of all the horror of hell, the blackness of its darkness whose obscurity is blacker than the most absolute blackness one can wildly imagine; it is so empty that nothing seems to be something and nonexistence seems to exist with an exasperating heaviness. I knew the insanity of hopelessness, and above all I knew the unforgettable, terrible, frightening absence of God.

"Hell is infinite in the prisons of the soul."[1]

There is a world of darkness as real as the one our eyes see,
and God has called us to tear down its gates and place it
under the footstool of the King of kings and Lord of lords.
This is His war cry: "Go ye and set them free!"

Back from the Brink

When the message of salvation was presented to me, I was completely demonized and recovering in a psychiatric hospital after having tried to commit suicide by cutting my veins. A pastor named, of all things, Christian, visited me. He had blue eyes, just as the Lord had told me would be the case in the vision I had when I was 18. The pastor spoke the good news gently to me, and I recognized that every word coming out of his mouth was the truth.

However, I started to weep; I told him: "What a terrible thing! You are preaching the salvation of my soul and I know what you have said is true; but in spite of everything I can't come to Christ. I have covenants which I cannot break. If I tried to, it would unleash all of the devil's anger on me. I cannot do anything."

In this moment of deep distress, the pastor interrupted me: "That is not true. The Word of God says, 'If we confess our sins, he is faithful and just and will forgive us our sins and purify us from all unrighteousness' [1 John 1:9]. Besides, the blood of Christ breaks every covenant. The Lord Jesus died for you to set you free from the chains of the devil."

These words created an earthquake within me. Without a shadow of doubt, the Holy Spirit was there performing a deep work in my soul. "What do I have to do to receive Jesus into my heart?" I asked, full of tears and with the sole desire that my beloved Jesus would put an end to this eternal nightmare.

"Repent," Pastor Christian replied, "and ask Him to come and live in you, telling Him you want Him to be your Lord and Savior."

"Repent" was the hardest and most difficult word he could have pronounced. But at that moment the Holy Spirit came upon me with such a conviction of sin that I fell to the floor, broken in a mixture of infinite pain and shame. It was a repentance that purged all my conscience. My soul literally poured itself out to God, crying out for His mercy. It was during this deep and sincere prayer that the Holy Spirit removed the veil from my eyes and I could see the deceit in which the devil had ensnared me and the terrible filthiness of my soul.

"Forgive me, Lord, forgive me," I said in a tiny voice. It was dreadful to think that God in His most beautiful purity could see the horrible person I had become. Nothing could make me feel more dirty or sadder at that time than I myself. I passionately desired to touch His impeccable kindness and to rid myself of everything that was keeping me away from His light.

Within me the demons became agitated with resentment and destruction. It was a heartrending fight in which my whole being took part. "Lord, tear out these worms, which are eating me up!" I desperately shouted within. I confessed my sins one by one, without any masks or pretenses. Weeping welled up from the deepest part of my soul. I saw how through serving the devil my actions nailed Jesus to the cross. Each one of my sins was a direct contradiction of the purity and holiness of Him who loved me in spite of everything and who gave His life for me.

No one has ever been so undeserving of God's grace, mercy and forgiveness than I. The purity of His presence was so strong that I felt like a vile worm before His divinity. I confessed, and the fire within consumed me. I deserved punishment and death more than this pretentious indulgence to which I aspired. "Lord!" I shouted, crumpled up in pain, "forgive me for daring to ask You for forgiveness. I am not worthy for You even to listen to me. But who apart from You is capable of having mercy on me? My Father, I am dying, I am totally broken on every side, and my heart is in pieces."

Then He started to fill me with His love. I clearly felt He was forgiving me. I could not believe there was a love so great that He would have compassion on me, a servant of Satan—but He did! Then, with all my being, I told Him, *"Thank You, Jesus!* Please come and live in my heart; cleanse me and take hold of my hand, so I will never leave You. Be my Lord and Savior."

While I was finishing speaking, the pastor laid his hands on my head and said, "Lord Jesus, I ask You to clean Your daughter Ana from all evil and to break every covenant she has made with the enemy."

Then I had the impression of seeing Jesus nailed to the cross and telling me He had done it because of His love for me, so I could be redeemed. It was so real I could almost touch it. I saw the blood flowing down His body and the weight of all the evil in the world causing deep pain in His soul. His blood was poured out to give me life, while on the other hand I had spilled my own blood to destroy myself.

Pastor Christian continued praying, "And I also ask that every evil spirit come out of Ana now and that the Holy Spirit fall upon her." With just these few simple words, in that precious moment, I felt as though a ray fell from heaven and broke every chain that was binding me. I felt the armor of suffering and oppression that had afflicted me shatter into a thousand pieces. An infinitely beautiful light filled the room; I felt the same marvelous goodness that I had felt when Christ visited me for the first time when I was a teenager. I felt like a bird, as though I could fly. My heart was filled with joy and peace, and I was absolutely certain of the fact that Christ had made me *free indeed.*

His glory remained in the room for hours as a shining glow; and when it dimmed and faded away, I was a new person, totally healed and delivered.

Plunging into Battle

From that morning I began to feel different. The crushed and depressed person the doctors had seen had been changed into a person full of enthusiasm who was oozing happiness through every pore. That depressing place full of peculiar people now presented itself as an open door through which to take my first steps in the way of the truth. A new conscience had awakened in my soul, and what could have been a very frustrating episode in my life, being confined with the mentally ill, now became a school where I learned how to communicate, from learning the simplest form of expression to coming to understand the cavernous concepts that move one's emotions.

During the days I remained in the hospital, God's presence was extremely strong over my life. The first thing the Holy Spirit told me was that I should not turn back in the slightest, because the enemy was greatly furious with my decision to follow Christ. Far from being afraid of these words, I became full of divine zeal; and I decided to go to war against the devil to the end, snatching from him all the souls I could, bringing to light his tricks, delivering the captives and serving God with all of my being, regardless of the devil's fury.

I felt blessed to be able to enter into these winding corridors of the human mind among people who had become so affected by Satan's cruelty that they had come to the point of losing their own identity. Many times I started to think about how the outside world could not even imagine the smallest part of what was happening there or of what one suffers or hallucinates. It is a world so far from our own that on discovering it and understanding it, it is a little like the sensation a child must have when he begins, by touching everything around him, to perceive the environment in which he lives.

In such an environment, at times a simple glance misinterpreted can unleash hell, and a word seemingly without significance can imprison someone for days. Judgment and parameters do not exist there. To come alongside or converse with its inhabitants requires subtlety and tact in their most delicate and sensitive forms. On occasions it was painful for me to listen to these people, and at other times it became a source of great enrichment.

There in the hospital God started to forge in me an indescribable love for the lost and for those tormented by the devil. It was also a good place to deal with my pride and vanity. There we all lost our individuality and personal recognition. We were all stamped with the same mark: "Psychiatric Patient." The same label was given to everyone, whether rich and famous or poor and unknown—each person was just that: one more person.

I saw people suffering pain so great that only the soul is capable of bearing it, because the body, being less resistant, could never survive it. When the heart screams, the cavity of your loneliness and your silence echoes it. It is absolute separation from all that surrounds us; it is the absence of hope, light and beauty.

Life in this setting is the cruel realization of our own smallness and helplessness. I frequently heard my fellow patients weeping as though their souls were being torn apart within, shrieking as though they were being gnawed and made to bleed from within. At that time nobody was willing to listen to them, caress them or speak to them with tender words. So they were locked up in a narrow room with four walls and no windows. They were constantly observed by a nurse peeking through a glass peephole. The walls were scratched and stained with blood. They became like caged animals. There was no mercy.

Through the years I have seen how the percentage of suicides, psychiatric illnesses and those oppressed by Satan has increased. Nobody wants to hear about them. They are so difficult to love. There they are, in pain, hiding behind their masks, many times occupying a pew in the church with nobody paying attention to them, rejected and misunderstood. But God hears the deafening cry of their souls day and night, and from His throne a horn of oil is being poured out with an authority that comes from God, birthed in the mercy and love of the Father. This is the same anointing that came upon the Lord Jesus when He said:

> The Spirit of the Lord is on me, because he has anointed me to preach good news to the poor. He has sent me to proclaim freedom for the prisoners and recovery of sight for the blind, to release the oppressed, to proclaim the year of the Lord's favor (Luke 4:18,19).

Speaking a Healing Word

One night while I was in the hospital, a few days after my conversion, God opened my eyes to the spiritual world surrounding me; and I saw how the devil had bound my fellow inmates and how he was torturing them like he had done with me. It grieved me so much. That night I prayed to God asking Him to do something and not to leave these people as they were.

The following morning when the pastor came to visit me, I told him what I had seen. And he read this passage to me:

> And these signs will accompany those who believe: In my name they will *drive out demons*; they will speak in new tongues; they will pick up snakes with their hands; and when they drink deadly poison, it will not hurt them at all; they will place their hands on sick people, and they will get well (Mark 16:17,18, emphasis added).

Suddenly this promise became alive within me; I believed as though I were a small child. "Let's go," I told the pastor. "Teach me how to do it! There is a woman who is suffering a lot, she shouts all the time and has been left paralyzed. Let's talk with her." Without losing any time, we entered the room of that sick woman. Christian, the pastor, preached the gospel to her; and we both laid hands on her.

I was very attentive, because I wanted to learn and not miss a single detail. Christian took authority and showed that he was very sure of what he was doing. He rebuked the evil spirit that was in the woman and ordered it to come out. He then took a small bottle of oil and anointed her as he proclaimed her healed. The woman remained as if sleeping after the prayer, so we left her room. I was expecting a full exorcism, but that did not happen. The pastor said good-bye and told me he would keep himself informed about the sick woman's condition.

The next morning I started to hear a great racket in the garden, so I went out to see what was disturbing the usual order and calm of the hospital. To my surprise, I saw the paralytic woman walking; she was in her right mind and completely healed, to the astonishment of everyone in the hospital. God was doing something that would lay the foundations of a solid faith in my life, as well as the groundwork for what would later be a key in casting out demons. Most of the patients were delivered in that psychiatric hospital during that time, until those who were in charge of the hospital forbade us to enter patients' rooms.

Implications for Deliverance Ministries

I do not intend to make this book a manual for personal deliverance. Wonderful books on this topic are already available. Yet

I should mention that I am becoming more convinced that deliverance is not a question of methods. For me, success in casting out demons depends upon four basic things: *authority* and *holiness* on the part of the deliverer and *repentance* and the *desire to be set free* on the part of the person who is possessed or tormented by demons (in cases where subjects are in control of their faculties).

Due to the background of my testimony and the strength of the satanic covenants I ignorantly made, many people imagine my deliverance to be somewhat spectacular—along the lines of Elaine (the witch set free by the Holy Spirit through Dr. Rebecca Brown), who for months faced terrible confrontations with demonic forces that beat and pursued her.[2] Far from that, my deliverance was extremely powerful and happened in a moment, although my experiences with the devil were very similar to those described by Elaine. The difference is that she was involved in Satanism and I was involved in Haitian Voodoo.

In this time of deep and progressive revelation of the Holy Spirit, God is giving us a practical, effective and balanced understanding of our organized fight against the forces of evil. During my own ministry I have seen the great indifference to the reality of the spiritual world in which people around us live. It is as though it does not exist. At times I am amazed at seeing such ignorance within the Church about the spiritual structures of evil and the effectiveness of the divine weapons God has placed in our hands.

I do not want to underrate any ministry, because I believe that in the search for the truth all have contributed something good to the Church with their teachings. It would be unjust to say they have not taught me anything. On the contrary, I have learned from them. However, two extremes in regard to the spiritual battle should be pointed out.

In one extreme, the devil is never mentioned, because it is believed that just to speak about Christ is to resolve everything and that there is no need to do anything more. Marvelous theology! But if this were true, why are there so many oppressed people and so many robbed by the devil within the Church? Why does the Bible contain so many military and battle terms that equip us for spiritual warfare? Why is the Lord called a "Man of War" (Exod. 15:3, *AMP*)? And why do we have weapons to pull down strongholds (see 2 Cor. 10:4)?

In the other extreme there are those who see demons behind every rock. They cannot carry on a peaceful conversation with each other without seeing countless demons leaping from their ears.

My own story, which seems to contradict all the books on deliverance that I have read, has been a strong testimony of faith and an encouragement for many to believe in the delivering power of Christ. I see in the Bible a determined and absolute action for casting out demons based on the authority that proceeds from the throne of God and in the knowledge of His Word. Deliverance should be something simple that every true believer can accomplish through the power of God. Is this not the case on the part of the Great Commission?

> Go into all the world and preach the good news to all creation. Whoever believes and is baptized will be saved, but whoever does not believe will be condemned. And these signs will accompany those who believe: In my name they will drive out demons; they will speak in new tongues; they will pick up snakes with their hands; and when they drink deadly poison, it will not hurt them at all; they will place their hands on sick people, and they will get well (Mark 16:15,16).

This is a gospel so simple and at the same time so powerful for those who can believe!

Notes

1. Torcuato Luca de Tena Benjumea, "The Endless Nightmare."
2. Rebecca Brown, *He Came to Set the Captives Free* (Monroeville, PA: Whitaker House Publishers, 1993).

CHAPTER 4

THE ORGANIZATION OF THE KINGDOM OF DARKNESS

The apostle Paul speaks of a battle in his letter to the Ephesians:

> Finally, be strong in the Lord and in his mighty power. Put on the full armor of God so that you can take your stand against the devil's schemes. For our struggle is not against flesh and blood, but against the rulers, against the authorities, against the powers of this dark world and against the spiritual forces of evil in the heavenly realms.

> And pray in the Spirit on all occasions with all kinds of prayers and requests. With this in mind, be alert and always keep on praying for all the saints (Eph. 6:10-12,18).

If we have to depend on *His mighty power*, if we have to put on *the full armor of God* and if we have to *always keep on praying*, this indicates to me that the Bible is not speaking about a simple little skirmish that, with a few short prayers and songs, is sufficient for us to live a peaceful Christian life. Yet this is what most children of God seem to believe. The fact is that the Spirit, through Paul, is speaking about a really important spiritual battle to establish the kingdom of God and tear down the gates of hell—which is the principal focus of the preaching of the gospel.

We have to understand that the devil *hates* God and His children and that he is going to do everything possible not only to keep the greatest number of souls in captivity but even to take the chosen into apostasy. The devil is in continual conflict with the kingdom of God, because what Satan wants is to sit on the throne of the Most High and be worshiped by men.

All truth is parallel. The Bible teaches that although the spiritual world is invisible, we see its effects in the natural world. The greater the demonic activity in a given country, then the greater poverty and the greater amount of crime, sin and corruption. Even the landscape is affected when demonic activity is very intense in the spiritual realm.

The spiritual sphere is made up of God and His angels on one side and by Satan and his demons on the other. The former live in the third heaven, where God's throne is located, where the apostle Paul was caught up to, and from whence angels have access to Earth where they carry out their service to the children of God. "Are not all angels ministering spirits sent to serve those who will inherit salvation?" (Heb. 1:14).

Since Satan is the prince of the air (see Eph. 2:2), he lives together with his hosts in what is known as the heavenly realms or second heaven (see Eph. 6:12). Here he builds strongholds of iniquity to govern from the air.

Another group exists within this kingdom of darkness. They are the fallen angels, who are held bound in the abyss to be released on judgment day. "And the angels who did not keep their positions of authority but abandoned their own home—these he has kept in darkness, bound with everlasting chains for judgment on the great Day" (Jude, v. 6). These willful spirit-beings are also referred to in the Book of Revelation:

> The fifth angel sounded his trumpet, and I saw a star that had fallen from the sky to the earth. The star was given the key to the shaft of the Abyss. When he opened the Abyss, smoke rose from it like the smoke from a gigantic furnace. The sun and sky were darkened by the smoke from the Abyss. And out of the smoke locusts came down upon the earth and were given power like that of scorpions of the earth (Rev. 9:1-3).

A third type of evil power consists of unclean spirits, or demons, who need a human body in which to live and work through. Since Satan is not omnipresent, he needs a structure of government in order to carry out his objectives.

Categories of the Demonic

Compare the apostle Paul's definitions and categories for this demonic hierarchy in Ephesians and Colossians:

Ephesians 6:12 *(KJV)*

(1) principalities
(2) powers
(3) rulers of darkness
(4) spiritual [hosts of] wickedness

Colossians 1:16 *(KJV)*

(1) thrones
(2) dominions
(3) principalities
(4) powers

Without making an extensive study of demonology, I want to analyze this kingdom of darkness so we can understand how it is organized and therefore be able to fight against it.

Thrones

The thrones imply a kingdom. A throne includes positions of rulership over one or more nations that have been manifested from generation to generation. In the natural world, when we speak of the throne of England, for example, we can visualize it as a conquering empire ruling all the nations under it that made up its colonies. Again, Daniel called Nebuchadnezzar, king of Babylon, "the king of kings": "You, O king, are the king of kings. The God of heaven has given you dominion and power and might and glory" (Dan. 2:37). And Isaiah referred to Babylon in this way: "Sit in silence, go into darkness, Daughter of the Babylonians; no more will you be called queen of kingdoms" (Isa. 47:5).

The same governance occurs in the spiritual realm, where thrones represent kingdoms that govern various countries. At times, God calls both Satan and some high-level spirits by the names of kings. For example, in the book of Isaiah, Lucifer is referred to as occupying the throne of Babylon (see Isa. 14:4,12,13, *KJV*); and in Daniel, the angel Michael fights against "the prince of the Persian kingdom" (Dan. 10:13).

I mention this because the Holy Spirit has already given us the strategies to do certain battles at a territorial level. We have prayed in places that were European colonies and that are now governed from thrones occupied by principalities such as the prince of Egypt, prince of Babylon, prince of Tyre, etc.

From the point of view of spiritual government, certain Latin-American cities and nations have the same characteristics as the great empires of times gone by, just as, in the natural world, colonies retain the traits of the nations that conquered them.

Writing on territorial spirits, Peter Wagner mentions a passage from the song of Moses in Deuteronomy 32:8: "When the Most High gave the nations their inheritance, when he divided all mankind, he set up boundaries for the peoples according to the number of the sons of Israel." Wagner comments:

> The problem comes with the expression "sons of Israel," which seems to have little to do with the governing of territories by spirits. However, scholars like F. F. Bruce tell us that thanks to certain discoveries made in the Dead Sea Scrolls which were found in cave number 4 of Qumran, we now know the version of the Septuagint (the Greek translation from Hebrew made some 250 years before the birth of Christ) represents the original text more accurately . . . The Septuagint informs us that God did it "according to the number of angels of God" . . . a crucial difference.[1]

The point is that in our time God is enabling Christians to participate in His warfare against evil spiritual forces. For example, a few years ago a prophecy ran through Christian circles around the world and many renowned prophets referred to it as something which definitely came from God. It was foretold for June 9, 1994, and was the fulfillment of the words in Isaiah 25:7:

"On this mountain he will destroy the shroud that enfolds all peoples, the sheet that covers all nations."

As it turned out, in the natural sphere there was an earthquake that day, early in the morning. It was 600 kilometers deep in the inner layers of the earth and measured an intensity of 9.0 on the Richter scale. But in the spiritual realm God allowed me to see something marvelous: The entire planet had been made bare, and around it I could see an incredible structure of edification that remained exposed. It was like an enormous range of construction works, very diverse but connected together at various points and resembling a gigantic mass of interconnected cities. Then, as a ray of light, the words of Psalm 18:15 came to me: "The valleys of the sea were exposed and the foundations of the earth laid bare at your rebuke, O LORD."

God is revealing from day to day the thrones that have to be pulled down to deliver the nations. For the first time, we are seeing the heavens uncovered—something many others in the past have wanted to see, but God has granted it to us.

Although much still remains to be discovered about this field of spiritual kingdoms and territories, the list of kingdoms cited in Jeremiah 25, where God speaks of the judgment of the nations, catches my attention. This is without a doubt a prophecy of the end times, but curiously the political division of the countries detailed there has nothing to do with the current political situation. Isn't God speaking of nations governed by spiritual kingdoms, rather than of political powers? And where in this spiritual description do all the nations of the earth fit?

Jeremiah tells us: "I took the cup from the LORD's hand and made all the nations to whom he sent me drink it: Jerusalem and the towns of Judah, its kings and officials, to make them a ruin" (25:17,18). What kings and officials are being spoken of in the actual state of Israel?

And note that verse 19 refers to "Pharaoh king of Egypt, his attendants, his officials and all his people." Who is this Pharaoh (who is called a "great monster" in Ezekiel 29:3)?

Then consider Jeremiah 25:20-26:

> And all the foreign people there; all the kings of Uz; all the kings of the Philistines (those of Ashkelon, Gaza, Ekron and the people left at Ashdod); Edom, Moab and Ammon; all the kings of Tyre and Sidon; the kings of the coastlands across the sea; Dedan, Tema, Buz and all who are in distant places; all the kings of Arabia and all the kings of the foreign people who live in the desert; all the kings of Zimri, Elam and Media; and all the kings of the north, near and far, one after the other—all the kingdoms on the face of the earth. And after all of them, the king of Sheshach will drink it too.

Who are all these kings? In a territorial battle that Pastor Harold Caballeros of Guatemala once undertook in his country, God showed him an enormous serpent passing through the nation. What it left behind was even seen in ruins in some parts of the capital. To guide Pastor Caballeros in creating a battle strategy, God gave him these Scriptures: Isaiah 14:29—"From the root of that snake will spring up a viper, its fruit will be a darting, venomous serpent"; and Isaiah 30:6—"An oracle concerning the animals of the Negev: Through a land of hardship and distress, of lions and lionesses, of adders and darting snakes."

Isn't this clearly the same spirit we see in northern Latin America known as Quetzalcoatl, the feathered serpent? The question which then arises is, Does the spiritual throne of the pharaoh of Egypt have anything to do with this Aztec god whose throne is surrounded by pyramids in Teotihuacan?

Hector Torres, in his book *Tearing Down Strongholds*, says:

> Mexico, Central America and South America are the cradle of the three most magnificent indigenous cultures, the Aztec, Maya and Inca. Archaeological studies and scientists seem to indicate there is a very close relationship between Mesopotamia, the center of Babylonian culture and Central America, even the cryptic symbols of the Maya and Babylonian cultures are very similar, like in the way they draw the eyes with preeminence given to the root of the snake, the flying dragon, etc.[2]

This confirms my belief that spiritual kingdoms exist that are not only assigned to a country or time but also embrace several nations throughout the centuries.

Dominions

In my opinion, this level of the demonic hierarchy is a power, as its name indicates; and as such it can have very diverse effects. I see dominions as spirits that bind kingdoms and that have dominion in many kingdoms without having one of their own. These are the ones that are over worldly organizations such as the United Nations, the European Community, OPEC, etc.

Dominions also include spirits that rule people all over the world through religions, philosophies such as New Age, humanism, etc., as well as sects and secret societies such as Masonry, Nazism and neo-Nazism (see the chapter on the diverse structures of strongholds).

A clear dominion that we have been fighting against in recent years is the queen of heaven, a male-female spirit that governs from the second heaven. This demonic force was first brought down to Earth during the time of the Tower of Babel. It is a complex spirit that operates through politics as well as religion, and it controls a great part of the wealth of the world.[3]

Principalities

Principalities are territorial spirits in charge of governing nations. Their work consists of adversely affecting the largest number of people possible. They operate in national misfortunes such as earthquakes, cyclones, mass suicides, mass poisonings, epidemics, etc. As an example, we have the prince of Persia and the prince of Greece against whom the archangel Michael fights in response to the fast of Daniel the prophet (see Daniel 10:13).

Powers

These are spirits that have been commissioned by Satan, forces of evil or branches of satanic power through which he stimulates, manipulates, seduces and controls certain sectors of the population, loosing over them specific types of sin. Here we find the powers of idolatry, witchcraft, prostitution, etc.

We have to understand that not all sins are governed by a power with the same name, but they are grouped under the dominion of a power, or strongman, who controls them. For example, there is not a power of witchcraft, another of sorcery and another of divination; but witchcraft is the demonic power through which Satan controls, dominates and manipulates man's will through various expressions. The power of witchcraft is thus going to mobilize the spirits under its command to control lives. It will move various spirits such as those of sorcery, spiritualism (those who move in mediums) and spirits of power (astral projection).

Rulers of Darkness

This category is in charge of governing influential people on the earth. These spirits are mostly assigned against ministers and leaders in the Church. For this reason it is important that we pray, as the apostle Paul told Timothy, for kings and all those in authority.

Spiritual Hosts of Wickedness

These are demonic legions assigned by the powers to provoke sin. They move in people such as witches and drug traffickers who influence and enslave others.

Unclean Spirits

Unclean spirits are the spirits that live in particular people or in places, such as houses or cemeteries. They also impregnate idols and objects with demonic character.

Notes

1. C. Peter Wagner, *Warfare Prayer* (Ventura, CA: Regal Books, 1992), p. 105.
2. Hector Torres, *Tearing Down Strongholds* (Miami, FL: Editorial Betania, 1993), p. 121.
3. See the excellent book *Confronting the Queen of Heaven* by Dr. C. Peter Wagner.

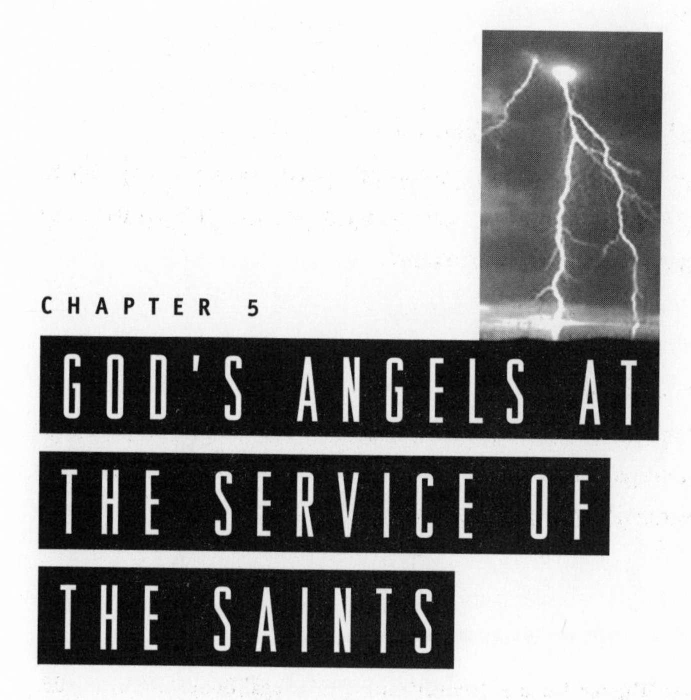

CHAPTER 5

GOD'S ANGELS AT THE SERVICE OF THE SAINTS

Without a doubt, nothing compares to finding oneself before the glorious presence of God, as we begin to experience the wonders of His kingdom. Little by little He reveals to us all He has for us, wanting us to absorb all that He is and to take possession of all the riches in the unequalled inheritance He has set aside for us.

Among these riches is the indescribable blessing of having the whole army of angels in heaven at our service. The epistle to the Hebrews asks: "To which of the angels did God ever say, 'Sit at my right hand until I make your enemies a footstool for your feet'? Are not all angels ministering spirits sent to serve those who will inherit salvation?" (Heb. 1:13,14).

The ability to see angels in any one given moment is one of the most exciting and powerful experiences we can have. I give glory to God for the innumerable times He has allowed me to fight alongside angels and see them come to my defense.

What does the Bible teach about these incomparable heavenly beings, these who are the hosts of the living God? For one thing, we know that millions of them exist. The apostle John reports: "Then I looked and heard the voice of many angels, numbering thousands upon thousands, and ten thousand times ten thousand. They encircled the throne and the living creatures and the elders" (Rev. 5:11).

Types of Angels

In one sense, angels are like all believers, in that they are created for the glory and praise of God. However, Scripture also teaches that there are various types of angels, each having different functions. Besides ministering in worship day and night before the throne of the Most High, they have been assigned unique tasks.

1. The Angel of the Lord

Although the first six books of the Old Testament speak numerous times about the Angel of the Lord, this is not an angel in the strict sense of the word. It is the title given to none other than Jesus Christ as He appeared and interacted with men before His coming in the flesh.

After Joshua had crossed the Jordan and circumcised the males among the people of God, the Angel of the Lord appeared before his eyes as a man:

> Now when Joshua was near Jericho, he looked up and saw a man standing in front of him with a drawn sword in his hand. Joshua went up to him and asked, "Are you for us or for our enemies?" "Neither," he replied, "but as commander of the army of the LORD I have now come." Then Joshua fell facedown to the ground in reverence, and asked him, "What message does my Lord have for his servant?" The commander of the LORD's army replied, "Take off your sandals, for the place where you are standing is holy." And Joshua did so (Josh. 5:13-15).

Here we see three important things. First, although no mere angel has ever legitimately accepted worship, this one did receive worship. Second, the only commander of the heavenly army is God Himself, and He identifies Himself as such. Third, He who appears here as a man speaks to Joshua the same words that Jehovah Himself spoke to Moses when He called to him from the burning bush, indicating that Jehovah and He are the same being and that the Angel of the Lord is a manifestation in angelic form of the Second Person of the Trinity.

2. Archangels

The English prefix "arch" is from the Greek word *archee,* meaning "principal," or "chief." Archangels are therefore the highest angels in a hierarchy of angels. Of these, the Bible refers to only one, Michael, by name, as in Jude verse 9: "But even the archangel

Michael, when he was disputing with the devil about the body of Moses . . ."

Michael is in charge of part of God's army of angels; and when fighting on behalf of Israel, he is identified as "your prince" (Dan. 10:21). Although scripturally he is the only one to receive this title, we know that other princes of God exist who could also fall in this category, for Daniel 10:13 refers to Michael as "one of the chief princes." Just as in the time of Daniel, Michael is now being sent into the fiercest battles the Church has ever fought to deliver the nations from the devil, who has enslaved them.

3. Cherubim

Members of this angelic order guard God's throne and His glory, as well as the tree of life which was in the Garden of Eden. After driving Adam and Even from the garden, God "placed on the east side of the Garden of Eden cherubim and a flaming sword flashing back and forth to guard the way to the tree of life" (Gen. 3:24).

King Hezekiah portrayed one of the duties of the cherubim when he prayed, "O LORD, God of Israel, enthroned between the cherubim, you alone are God over all the kingdoms of the earth" (2 Kings 19:15). In the same way as the throne of God in heaven is surrounded by cherubim, the Ark of the Testimony in the most holy place and the curtains of the tabernacle were decorated with figures of these heavenly beings.

Psalm 18:10 depicts God as manifesting His presence while riding on the cherubim: "He mounted the cherubim and flew; he soared on the wings of the wind."

Throughout Ezekiel 10 the cherubim, which the Bible also calls "living creatures" (v. 15), undergirded God's glory and moved in unison with Him whenever the glory moved.

Satan himself, in his time, was one of the cherubim, the most beautiful and perfect creature God created, and Satan was in charge of all the praise in heaven:

> You were anointed as a guardian cherub, for so I ordained you. You were on the holy mount of God; you walked among the fiery stones. You were blameless in your ways from the day you were created till wickedness was found in you (Ezek. 28:14,15).

The Bible does not describe this type of angelic host as having direct contact with man, except for Satan in his current, fallen state.

4. Seraphim

Another type of angel is the seraphim. These angels are mentioned only in the book of the prophet Isaiah:

> In the year that King Uzziah died, I saw the Lord seated on a throne, high and exalted, and the train of his robe filled the temple. Above him were seraphs [Heb. *seraphim*, plural], each with six wings: With two wings they covered their faces, with two they covered their feet, and with two they were flying (Isa. 6:1,2).

The difference between the seraphim and the cherubim is that the seraphim are above the throne and the cherubim are under it.

Seraphim can draw near to people and minister to them directly, carrying out God's orders and speaking to them:

> Then one of the seraphs flew to me with a live coal in his hand, which he had taken with tongs from the altar.

> With it he touched my mouth and said, "See, this has touched your lips; your guilt is taken away and your sin atoned for" (Isa. 6:6,7).

5. Guardian Angels

The rest of the angels, although having different functions, power and size, are not given any other name apart from the term "angels." Some are popularly known as guardian angels, primarily from Matthew 18:10, where Jesus indicates that an angel is assigned to every infant who is born and each guardian angel takes care of that child throughout their lives: "See that you do not look down on one of these little ones. For I tell you that their angels in heaven always see the face of my Father in heaven."

The Function of Angels

Scripture gives us occasional glimpses of the work and function of angels—portrayals that should serve to encourage believers about how our heavenly Father often works through angelic beings behind the scenes on our behalf.

Angels Celebrate in Heaven

> In the same way, I tell you, there is rejoicing in the presence of the angels of God over one sinner who repents (Luke 15:10).

They Accompany Believers to Paradise

> The time came when the beggar died and the angels carried him to Abraham's side. The rich man also died and was buried (Luke 16:22).

They Write in the Books of the Great Judgment

> Then He cried out in my hearing with a loud voice saying, "Draw near, O executioners of the city, each with his destroying weapon in his hand." And behold, six men came from the direction of the upper gate which faces north, each with his shattering weapon in his hand; and among them was a certain man clothed in linen with a writing case at his loins. And they went in and stood beside the bronze altar (Ezek. 9:1,2, *NASB*).

> And I saw the dead, great and small, standing before the throne, and books were opened. Another book was opened, which is the book of life. The dead were judged according to what they had done as recorded in the books (Rev. 20:12).

They Are Commissioned to Execute Judgment

God sends angels to execute judgment on people, cities and nations:

> Do not let your mouth lead you into sin. And do not protest to the temple messenger, "My vow was a mistake." Why should God be angry at what you say and destroy the work of your hands? (Eccles. 5:6).

> As I listened, he said to the [angels], "Follow him through the city and kill, without showing pity or compassion" (Ezek. 9:5).

> I saw in heaven another great and marvelous sign: seven angels with the seven last plagues–last, because with them God's wrath is completed (Rev. 15:1).

Angels Bring God's Messages to People

I asked, "What are these, my lord?" The angel who was talking with me answered, "I will show you what they are" (Zech. 1:9).

Angels Bring Physical Sustenance to God's Children

Then [Elijah] lay down under the tree and fell asleep. All at once an angel touched him and said, "Get up and eat." He looked around, and there by his head was a cake of bread baked over hot coals, and a jar of water. He ate and drank, and then lay down again (1 Kings 19:5,6).

Angels Provide Spiritual Strength

"Father, if you are willing, take this cup from me; yet not my will, but yours be done." An angel from heaven appeared to him and strengthened him (Luke 22:42,43).

Angels Rescue People from Chains and Imprisonment

Suddenly an angel of the Lord appeared and a light shone in the cell. He struck Peter on the side and woke him up. "Quick, get up!" he said, and the chains fell off Peter's wrists (Acts 12:7).

Angels Guard the Way of the Just

If you make the Most High your dwelling—even the LORD, who is my refuge—then no harm will befall you,

> no disaster will come near your tent. For he will command his angels concerning you to guard you in all your ways (Ps. 91:9-11).

Angels Are Our Allies in the Task of Disarming Satan

> Then [the angel] continued, "Do not be afraid, Daniel. Since the first day that you set your mind to gain understanding and to humble yourself before your God, your words were heard, and I have come in response to them" (Dan. 10:12).

Experiences with Angels

Angels have a different task from that of the Holy Spirit. While the Spirit has the job of revealing Christ to men, angels are engaged in ministering spiritual and material goods, fighting battles and arranging circumstances.

Angelic Appearances: Glory and Warning

Angels may or may not physically appear to human eyes. At times they resemble human beings, as when Abraham received the angels who told him of their plan to destroy Sodom and Gomorrah:

> The LORD appeared to Abraham near the great trees of Mamre while he was sitting at the entrance to his tent in the heat of the day. Abraham looked up and saw three men standing nearby. When he saw them, he hurried

from the entrance of his tent to meet them and bowed low to the ground (Gen. 18:1,2).

They can also be seen in their real form, in their heavenly beauty, with unfolded wings and robes of light—as those whom Jacob saw at Bethel when, through a dream, God showed him the spiritual world. Jacob "had a dream in which he saw a stairway resting on the earth, with its top reaching to heaven, and the angels of God were ascending and descending on it" (Gen. 28:12).

Angels are creatures of such magnificence and beauty that man's natural reaction is to fall down and worship them. This was the apostle John's experience on the island of Patmos during his visions, which are in the book of Revelation. However, the Word is very clear in commanding that only God should be worshiped and given adoration:

> I, John, am the one who heard and saw these things. And when I had heard and seen them, I fell down to worship at the feet of the angel who had been showing them to me. But he said to me, "Do not do it! I am a fellow servant with you and with your brothers the prophets and of all who keep the words of this book. Worship God!" (Rev. 22:8,9).

Also, Paul writes in the epistle to the Colossians:

> Let no one defraud you by acting as an umpire and declaring you unworthy and disqualifying you for the prize, insisting on self-abasement and worship of angels, taking his stand on visions [he claims] he has seen, vainly puffed up by his sensuous notions and inflated by his unspiritual thoughts and fleshly conceit (2:18; *AMP*).

An angel's beauty should never be taken as an indication of that angel's relationship with God, as demonic angels are able to disguise themselves as angels of light to deceive. It is the angels' message that shows us whether they come from the kingdom of God or the kingdom of darkness. Paul tells us: "But even if we or an angel from heaven should preach a gospel other than the one we preached to you, let him be eternally condemned!" (Gal. 1:8).

Satan is always looking for worship, just like his followers. Millions of people who have given themselves to idolatry have fallen into this grave error, sometimes by following assumed appearances of virgins who were actually demonic angels dressed in light, looking for temples of worship to be built in their honor—"and no wonder, for Satan himself masquerades as an angel of light" (2 Cor. 11:14).

It is important that we be extremely careful that our spiritual life does not depend upon angels. Neither should our prayers be directed to them in order to solicit their favor.

We depend upon God, to whom alone we direct our petitions; and it is He who decides whether to send His army for our service.

A correct prayer would be something like this:

> Lord, I put myself in Your hands, because You alone are my strong rock and strong tower. All my trust is in You. Father, I now ask You to send Your angels to guard me and to fight against every evil spirit that wants to attack me.

Angels Versus Witches

Angels are extremely useful in battles against the devil, especially when we have to fight with human spirits. When dealing with ing demons, we as Christians have the authority to tread on serpents and scorpions, and according to our faith, we will sooner or later cast them out (see Luke 10:19). The problem occurs in deliverance or in a territorial battle where the spirits of witches interfere.

The Bible tells us that the demons believe in God and tremble when they hear His name. Men, however, often do not believe nor do they fear or obey the name of Christ. This causes a problem for us—while demons obey, the spirits of witches do not.

What shall we do then? On one occasion, when we were engaged in an enormous battle trying to deliver a young woman who had practiced witchcraft, the Lord revealed to us that the demons had left but that spirits of witches were fighting for her soul, keeping her bound. I clearly heard the Holy Spirit telling me to ask for angels to take the witches away in chains and to speak to them of their defeat before the power of Jesus Christ. No sooner had I prayed when two enormous angels appeared beside the woman; they captured the spirits of the witches and took them away, and the young woman smiled in total freedom.

Events Angelic and Glorious

On another occasion, angels appeared to several people while we were taking prayer warriors to the pyramids of Teotihuacan. We had divided into two groups. One group climbed up the pyramid of the sun. On their way up, they were attacked by terrible spirits of fear who almost paralyzed them. They started to pray, to rebuke the spirits with all their strength and to ask God for angels to come to aid in the battle. In this moment, four beautiful angels, each 12 feet tall, took up positions like sentinels with great power, standing on the four corners of the highest part of the pyramid.

The atmosphere changed completely. An incredible mantle of God's peace came upon the group, and they were able to break all the covenants and sacrifices that had been made to the ancestral gods. On finishing, the Lord crowned their victory with a precious, round rainbow of seven colors shining on the apex of the fallen throne of Quetzalcoatl. Praise be to the King of kings and Lord of lords!

Angels have opened doors for us to enter into the most unusual places. Once I traveled to the United States without a passport. God sent His angels and allowed me to enter the country anyway. In another instance, I was enabled by God to board an airplane that had a waiting list of more than 40 people—God sent an angel who saw to it that I got on board.

Angels help in other ways, too. We have been delivered from death on several occasions by angels. Once a whole town came after us. They even had stones and sticks to kill us, but God's angelic army dispersed them. In another situation, we have seen angels come down and worship with us in glorious services of praise to God.

I could almost write another book on the numerous, wonderful experiences God has allowed us to have with angels. Some of them I have recounted in the last chapters of this book.

Our prayer every day is for the Lord Jesus to surround our house and the homes of our relatives and members of the Church with angels to guard us and watch over our sleep.

For those whose joy is prayer, whose delight is to be before the throne of the Most High, whose lives are so entwined with the kingdom of God that they are one with His will, being with angels is a part of everyday life. Jesus had this experience in mind for us when He prayed in deep intercession for all those who would believe in His name, knowing that "they are not of the world, even as I am not of it" (John 17:16).

CHAPTER 6

AUTHORITY OVER THE POWER OF THE ENEMY

While giving an extraordinary conference on spiritual warfare in my country, Dr. Rony Chaves explained the deep meaning of the word "authority" and how essential it is to understand this concept in facing the devil in battle.

Dr. Chaves pointed out that the word comes from the Greek *exousia*, a term that is used to express the maximum authority of God. It is the word Christ used when He said, "All authority in heaven and on earth has been given to me" (Matt. 28:18).

"Exousia" comes from two words–*ex*, which means "from out of" and *ousia*, which means "being within," or "through." This describes the way through which Jesus came in human form, entering man's environment and limiting himself as a human. So Jesus came "from out of" (ex) the Father, bringing with Him the "being within" (ousia), that is, the maximum authority flowing from the Father and thus powerful enough to destroy the works of hell. This same term is used when Jesus gives authority to His followers over demonic powers (see Mark 3:15). Christ is glorified by the Father with a name that is above every other name in heaven, on the earth and under the earth. Jesus has received the authority and the Kingdom; He is now telling the Church that in the same way the Father worked in Him, He is now working in us. Christ, who came from out of the Father, is seated in majesty at the right hand of the Father; but being within us through the Spirit, He is making his authority flow through us, performing miracles and wonders in us and filling us with power.[1]

Referring to this, we read of the authority we have in Christ: "And God raised us up with Christ and seated us with him in the heavenly realms in Christ Jesus" (Eph. 2:6). The Early Church understood this power, and the works of the devil were destroyed. Demons were cast out, the sick healed, the dead raised.

The Power and the Glory

The authority of God has to do with the essence of who God is. He is the King of kings and Lord of lords. He is the creator.

> He is the image of the invisible God, the firstborn over all creation. For by him all things were created: things in heaven and on earth, visible and invisible, whether thrones or powers or rulers or authorities; all things were created by him and for him. He is before all things, and in him all things hold together (Col. 1: 15-17).

Jesus is the Word present from the beginning. He was with God, and He was God (see John 1:1). He spoke in the power of His authority, and matter crossed over from the limits of the invisible realm to become visible. In the beginning, when God rearranged the earth, which was formless and empty, when everything was in darkness and the Spirit of God moved over the face of the waters, Jesus, in the voice of the omnipotent One, uttered *Fiat lux* ("Let there be light" [Gen. 1:3]). Darkness could not stay, and chaos was absorbed by life.

This authority that had the power to bring order over a confused and disorderly creation, arranging it and giving it life, also miraculously shined His light among men. "In him was life, and that life was the light of men. The light shines in the darkness, but the darkness has not understood it" (John 1:4,5). So Jesus also has authority over the disordered mass of sickness, bringing life to it as well. He has power over the disorder of empty families, bringing life and light to them.

Ultimate power is not in the hands of cancer or adultery or drugs or the devil. *God has the power!* In the beginning, His authority made the wind blow, and like a stormy gust the waters were divided. The clouds of vapor were gathered up to the heavens. The prophet Jeremiah describes this:

> He made the earth by his power; he founded the world by his wisdom and stretched out the heavens by his

understanding. When he thunders, the waters in the heavens roar; he makes clouds rise from the ends of the earth. He sends lightning with the rain and brings out the wind from his storehouses (Jer. 51:15,16).

He sent His word in authority and separated the waters from the dry land. He set boundaries for the surface of the seas and ordered them not to cross over:

The voice of the LORD is over the waters; the God of glory thunders, the LORD thunders over the mighty waters. The voice of the LORD is powerful; the voice of the LORD is majestic. The voice of the LORD strikes with flashes of lightning. The voice of the LORD shakes the desert. The LORD sits enthroned over the flood; the LORD is enthroned as King forever. *The LORD gives strength to his people* (Ps. 29:3,4,7,8,10,11, emphasis added).

This is the same authority the Son of God moved in when He calmed the storm. His disciples asked, "Who is this? He commands even the winds and the water, and they obey him" (Luke 8:25).

Job spoke about this authority:

The pillars of the heavens quake, aghast at his rebuke. By his power he churned up the sea; by his wisdom he cut Rahab to pieces. And these are but the outer fringe of his works; how faint the whisper we hear of him! Who then can understand the thunder of his power? (Job 26:11,12,14).

His voice resounded in the heavens and the firmament unfolded. He thundered again from on high, and the stars in the sky lit up like an infinite flash of light. Life, the essence of Christ, covered the earth and His voice gave it form, filling the seas with fish and the sky with birds. In His wisdom, He created Adam and breathed His Spirit into him and gave him dominion over all the earth.

Power Abdicated

Choosing to believe the terrible lie that he could be like God, Adam betrayed the Lord in an act of sin and gave the devil dominion over the world. The Earth became sick; out of it came thorns and thistles. The curse was upon it. Flesh became ill and mortal. The Spirit of the eternal had withdrawn from men.

The devil lashed out; the Earth became filled with iniquity, bringing destruction and death. Satan's seed of evil grew in each man and each woman who came into the world.

Grieved by the evil of mankind, God destroyed the earth with a flood. However, He did not destroy the entire human race but chose Noah and his family (eight people), who still believed and worshiped Him, to repopulate the world. God's purposes, plans and supreme authority were going to prevail—no matter what the devil did, no matter what man did, try as they might.

Power Enfleshed

Then one day the event occurred that would change the history of humanity: God Himself took the form of a human to live among us and to save us from eternal death. Thus the Word, the Son of the living God, decided to humble Himself to the uttermost by coming to Earth in the form of a man:

> And the Word (Christ) became flesh (human incarnate) and tabernacled (fixed His tent of flesh, lived awhile) among us; and we [actually] saw His glory (His honor,

> His majesty), such glory as an only begotten son receives from his father, full of grace (favor, loving-kindness) and truth (John 1:14, *AMP*).

God made His tabernacle flesh, so flesh would receive the glory of the Father. He made His dwelling place flesh, so flesh would be the dwelling place of His Spirit. He made the flesh His home, so flesh would receive the power of the Omnipotent, so life could be manifested in flesh, so life would absorb mortality and reclothe the flesh in immortality. The Hebrew writer stated it thus:

> Since the children have flesh and blood, he too shared in their humanity so that by his death he might destroy him who holds the power of death—that is, the devil—and free those who all their lives were held in slavery by their fear of death (Heb. 2:14,15).

Insomuch as the children have been cursed, He Himself became cursed. Insomuch as the children partook in sickness, He carried our sicknesses in His body:

> Surely he took up our infirmities and carried our sorrows, yet we considered him stricken by God, smitten by him, and afflicted. But he was pierced for our transgressions, he was crushed for our iniquities; the punishment that brought us peace was upon him, and by his wounds we are healed (Isa. 53:4,5).

His blood was shed. The ark in heaven was covered with His blood. The Father accepted His blood. And Jesus descended into hell, having paid the price. Sheol was filled with the presence of the Lord. The decrees and curses which were against us were left nailed to the Cross.

Satanic Power Overcome

With Christ's supreme act on the cross, the principalities and powers of Satan were disarmed. He confronted the prince of darkness, and the devil could not face him. Satan fell demolished, destroyed. The Lord was victorious over the devil's throne. Through death He destroyed him who held the power of death! Jesus snatched the keys to hades from Satan, robbing him of all authority over man. What Jesus had seen when He was still with His disciples had been fulfilled: "I saw Satan fall like lightning from heaven" (Luke 10:18). And fallen he remained, defeated at the feet of Christ.

Jesus has triumphed; Jesus has overcome!

At this moment, the force of God's all-powerful Spirit began to shake hell. Life, like a most powerful beam of fire, entered Jesus' dead body. His muscles started to react; His feet began to move. The wonder of life in that tomb shook the foundations of the principalities and powers. The angels, as fierce lightning, came down to remove the stone.

Hell could not hold Him; death could not keep Him; the tomb could not contain Him; He arose having won our victory. The heavens saw it; the Father saw it; and the devil saw it, heard it, felt it and experienced it at the very core of his being!

Hallelujah, glory to God in the highest, glory to Him who lives and reigns and will never be overcome, to Jesus Christ, our Savior, in whom we live and move and have our being. Praise to

God for the authority of Jesus Christ, who made the heavens and the earth, who has a name above every other name and at whose name every knee must bow, in heaven, on the earth and under the earth.

The devil has never had that authority and he never will! The devil does not have the power, *Jesus has the power;* your sickness does not have the power, *Jesus has the power*; your pain does not have the power, *Jesus has the power;* your vices do not have the power, *Jesus has the power*; the adultery that is breaking up your home does not have the power, *Jesus has the power.*

And we have been told that in His authority *we* have the authority to "drive out demons . . . speak in new tongues . . . pick up snakes . . . drink deadly poison [and] it will not hurt" (Mark 16:17,18).

Jesus has given us the power. You now have the power to undo the works of the devil (see 1 John 3:8)!

Satan's Strategy of Doubt and Fear

For too long the Church has lived in defeat, because although in its mind, doctrinally, it knows the devil is defeated, deep down there are strongholds of doubt created by demons. They frighten the believer, portraying Satan as an enormously powerful being who causes the earth to shake with terror and who destroys everything in his path. With such power, nobody wants to be face-to-face with him, not even for a second.

This is the greatest lie. The devil is effectively overcome, but his snare is to make us believe he still has power. The apostle Paul writes about the antichrist's subtlety in wielding his tricks.

He is "the one whose coming is in accord with the activity of Satan, with all power and signs and false wonders" (2 Thess. 2:9, *NASB*). Such so-called power was overcome by Christ on the cross, and now, "When he comes, he will convict the world of guilt in regard to sin and righteousness and judgment . . . because the prince of this world now stands condemned" (John 16: 8,11).

The Holy Spirit is assuring the Church that the devil is smashed to pieces, crushed and crumbled. Therefore we can stand up with confidence in the war against the devil. Our victory will depend on our knowing "that in the middle of the battle the devil is defeated."[2]

Speaking of the person who is born of God, John says that "God keeps him safe, and the evil one cannot harm him" (1 John 5:18). And again, "I write to you, young men, because you are strong, and the word of God lives in you, and you have overcome the evil one" (1 John 2:14).

Satan's only power is to lie, because he is the father of lies. It is his way of causing us to believe that he is some monstrous, powerful being, when in fact he is only going around making the most incredibly deceitful parodies. He is going to present you with an absolutely terrible situation so that you lose strength until you become discouraged. The writer of Hebrews says to "consider him who endured such opposition from sinful men, so that you will not grow weary and lose heart" (Heb. 12:3).

Satan's objective is to make us discouraged. He is going to show you false diagnoses through X-ray images. The same spirit that makes figures appear in crystal balls also makes tumors and other anomalies appear—but this is no more than the lying work of Satan's hands. He is going to try to frighten you by putting obstacles in front of everything you want to do for God. He is going to deny permits you need; he is going to erase you from passenger lists; he is going to interfere with the engine of your car; he will threaten to kill you. *But all such works are lies!*

The Elijah Complex

One of the passages of Scripture that clearly shows us this false and intimidating power of Satan is 1 Kings 19:2, which describes Queen Jezebel's sending a messenger to Elijah the prophet after he had caused the priests of Baal to be killed: "So Jezebel sent a messenger to Elijah to say, 'May the gods deal with me, be it ever so severely, if by this time tomorrow I do not make your life like that of one of them.'"

Yet Elijah acted as too many Christians do: "He came to a broom tree, sat down under it and prayed that he might die. 'I have had enough, LORD,' he said. 'Take my life; I am no better than my ancestors'" (vv. 4,5).

Elijah fell into the devil's great game of lies. He wanted to show the Lord that he was a victim and that no matter how much he fought, nothing could match Jezebel's terrible power. Having this Elijah complex, many Christians seek pastoral counsel only to unburden their souls and show the pastor that their real problems do not have solutions, because God does not hear them.

What Elijah did not know was that the Lord would yet use him to anoint prophets and kings; Elijah did not know that 7,000 of his countrymen had not bowed to Baal or that even Jezebel would soon be eaten by dogs.

If we would only trust that behind each difficult circumstance God has a glorious plan, one that is much greater than we can imagine!

God has taught me a great truth in the fight against the devil: Everything that we give importance to has power over us. If Satan manages to keep us worried, discouraged, sad and in defeat, he is doing so because we give him authority over us. And in doing so, we are arranging for him to be the one taking the glory, instead of Christ.

Sadness tells God "You can't do it!" Defeat tells God "You don't have power!" Negativism tells God "You can't!" Worry tells God "You don't love me!"

Complaints are the sound of hell! Praise is the sound of the kingdom of God!

Jesus said, "But understand this: If the owner of the house had known at what hour the thief was coming, he would not have let his house be broken into" (Luke 12:39). Every time we walk with destructive thoughts, we are walking on the devil's ground. We are letting him sow seeds of defeat in our heart; we are letting him break into our house. The Lord tells us: "Above all else, guard your heart, for it is the wellspring of life" (Prov. 4:23). He also tells us:

> For the weapons of our warfare are not physical [weapons of flesh and blood], but they are mighty before God for the overthrow and destruction of strongholds, [inasmuch as we] refute arguments and theories and reasonings and every proud and lofty thing that sets itself up against the [true] knowledge of God; and we lead every thought and purpose away captive into the obedience of Christ, (the Messiah, the Anointed One)" (2 Cor. 10:4,5, *AMP).*

Many say, "I don't know how to fight; I get easily confused when the devil attacks my thoughts." Remember that the people of Israel were slaves, not warriors, when they came out of Egypt. The first thing God showed them was, not how to wield the sword, but how to see Him through the column of fire and the pillar of cloud that led them away from Pharaoh and toward the Promised Land.

So the Lord is also saying to us:

> *I have not put the responsibility of the battle in any man's hands. All power is given unto Me, and I am delegating that power to you.*

"For the LORD your God is the one who goes with you to fight for you against your enemies to give you victory" (Deut. 20:4).

Understanding Who We Are

This principle has tremendous power, but it won't begin to work until our will decides to put it into action. God's authority has to be exercised by believers. We have to know who we are in Jesus Christ.

The apostle Paul prayed that we might have a deep understanding of the infinite power that would come upon the believers:

> [For I always pray to] the God of our Lord Jesus Christ, the Father of glory, that He may grant you a spirit of wisdom and revelation [of insight into mysteries and secrets] in the [deep and intimate] knowledge of Him, by having the eyes of your heart flooded with light, so that you can know and understand the hope to which He has called you, and how rich is His glorious inheritance in the saints (His set-apart ones), *And [so that you can know and understand] what is the immeasurable and unlimited and surpassing greatness of His power in and for us who believe* (Eph. 1:17-19, *AMP*, emphasis added).

To doubt that this immeasurable power dwells in us is to doubt Christ's own power. So Paul asserts this truth:

> As demonstrated in the working of His mighty strength, which He exerted in Christ when He raised Him from the dead and seated Him at His [own] right hand in the heavenly [places], far above all rule and authority and power and dominion and every name that is named [above every title that can be conferred], not only in this age and in this world, but also in the age and the world which are to come. And He has put all things under His feet and has appointed Him the universal and supreme Head of the church [a headship exercised throughout the church], which is His body, the fullness of Him Who fills all in all [for in that body lives the full measure of Him Who makes everything complete, and Who fills everything everywhere with Himself] (Eph. 1:19-23, *AMP*).

Too many Christians live with Hollywood's idea of the devil as an extremely powerful being who is able to beat the Christians at his fancy. I am grieved to see so many Christians living defeated, robbed and sick lives, having tremendous financial problems and complaining to every person they meet about their ill fortune. Beloved reader, we must understand with every cell of our being who we really are in Christ and that in Him we have total authority over the forces of the devil.

Enough of paying attention to every lie the devil wants to put in your head!

A Personal Lesson

Once I found myself crying in my bed, sick, without money, without work and inconsolable. "How long, Lord, how long?" I started to cry out from my bed of pain, just like Job. Then I heard the voice of the Lord, furious and thundering in my room. Filled with panic I sat up, not knowing why God could be angry with a poor victim like me. He then told me:

Get up, I have not called you to be lying in bed, I have given you my power to heal the sick, so go and do it!

Later He added,

Neither have I called you to remain inconsolable. I have given you power to make wealth, so you can extend your hand to the poor and do My work. Get up and give. And lastly, go and comfort My people by the power and the love of My Spirit whom I have placed in you.

I remained speechless, unable to blink from the shame. Five minutes later, a sister who was seriously ill knocked on the door, asking me to pray for her. I found new courage in God and prayed in His strength. The Spirit descended powerfully and healed both of us.

After half an hour, someone in financial need came; and I gave him all that I had, perhaps the equivalent of $5. A little later the telephone rang, and it was another person in distress. I ministered Christ's love to her, and the super-abundant peace of His presence came over her.

In the evening as I was rejoicing in what was one of the most important lessons of my life, someone knocked on the door again. I opened it; and there was a man I didn't know, holding an envelope. He gently smiled, asked if I was Ana Méndez, then gave it to me and turned around and left. In that envelope there was approximately $500 with no letter, not even the name or address of the sender. God in His faithfulness had sent the man to me; I knew he was an angel.

God was doing something important in my life. He was not only teaching me how to live a victorious life but also equipping me to confront the gates of hell.

The Pattern of Victory

God has taught me other great lessons in my spiritual life, following the framework and pattern of Jesus' ministry.

At the noble moment when He was baptized, the Father and the Holy Spirit appeared together with the Son, as Jesus was about to enter the waters. He was not baptized for the forgiveness of sins, of course, but to establish the Body of which He would become the Head and which would be made up of all those who are baptized in Him. In that historic moment, the glory of God was seen, the all-powerful voice of the Father was heard to the amazement of the people listening, and the Holy Spirit descended upon Jesus in the form of a dove.

Full of the Spirit, Jesus began His ministry in the desert with the famous confrontation with Satan himself. Why? Because it was important that He learn how to triumph over the devil during His ministry. In a similar way, whatever our ministry, in order to be overcomers in our Christian lives, we must establish our position before the enemy of our souls. Jesus stood face-to-face with the devil and decreed that the eternal Father is the One who has the power and that Satan had no power over Him. Because we are His, we too are overcomers when we minister in His power.

In the next chapter, we will explore the anointing Christ received in the wilderness and how that anointing can also rest on us.

Notes

1. Dr. Rony Chaves, Mexicans in Victory conference, April 1994.
2. Morris Cerullo, New Anointing video series.

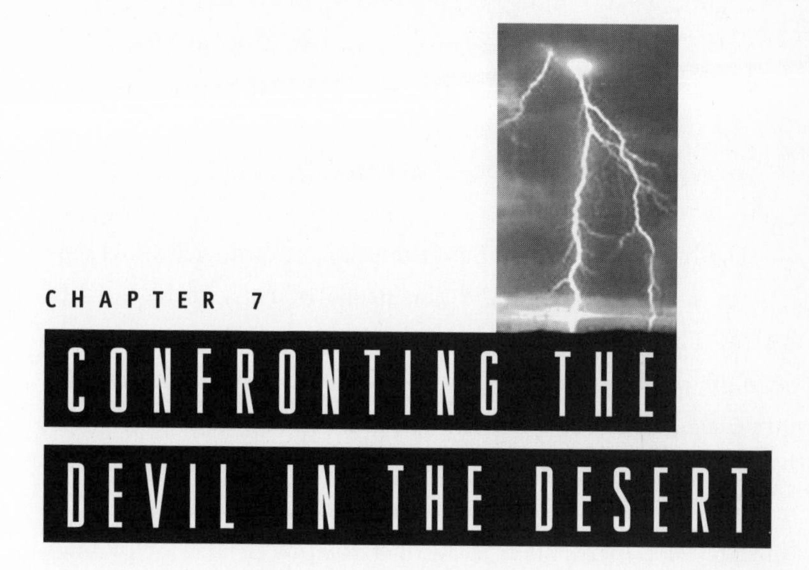

CHAPTER 7

CONFRONTING THE DEVIL IN THE DESERT

As we engage in spiritual warfare and seek the anointing that enables us to overcome Satan, we can learn no more valuable lessons than those that are revealed in Christ's confrontation with him in the wilderness. It is important that we begin at this point, in the desert, because we must understand that the empowerment we seek does not come in the context of comfort but in the crucible of confrontation.

Sustenance from Another World

Matthew records the first round in this great battle between Christ and the tempter in these words:

> Then Jesus was led by the Spirit into the desert to be tempted by the devil. After fasting forty days and forty nights, he was hungry. The tempter came to him and said, "If you are the Son of God, tell these stones to become bread." Jesus answered, "It is written: 'Man does not live on bread alone, but on every word that comes from the mouth of God'" (Matt. 4:1-4).

The bread with which Satan tempts the famished Jesus represents sustenance, life and the needs of this world—earthly desires. This first temptation, which is also our first temptation, is to live in accordance with the laws and the desires of this world rather than conform to the kingdom of God.

Jesus established the beginning of a spiritual kingdom in the midst of this earthly realm. It was a kingdom not governed by human deficiencies such as hunger for literal food or by laws with earthly limitations. Christ's kingdom is governed by the creative Word of God.

Thus, in resisting the devil's overtures, Jesus is decreeing that the Word of God is the supreme authority in His life. He has made the decision to defeat Satan out of spiritual resources instead of being defeated by the temptation to rely on fleshly sustenance. In making this choice, Jesus shows His willingness to live by principles that are totally contradictory to the natural laws. He is decreeing that His life is absolutely sustained and protected by the Word of God.

The first step to victory is, therefore, to determine in our hearts and to let the devil know that we live and depend 100 percent on God's Word, which is infallible, all-powerful, unlimited and eternal. This must not be a choice based merely on something dogmatic or on the Word's being engraved in our memory; rather, it must be based on the fact that the Word is impregnated in our spirit, it is knowledge revealed to the deepest parts of our being. We confront Satan successfully only when we know in our soul that heaven and Earth will pass away but that God's Word will never pass away.

You are under a curse if you still think that your sustenance depends on your own strength or on material resources. Remember that God cursed man as He expelled Adam and Eve from the garden and told them, "By the sweat of your brow you will eat your food" (Gen. 3:19). Of course, "Christ redeemed us from the curse of the law by becoming a curse for us, for it is written: 'Cursed is everyone who is hung on a tree'" (Gal. 3:13). But if you persist on depending on this world's sustenance, remaining under the curse, the devil will eat the dust that you are; he will steal from you; and he will devour your sown land, because you will be sowing between thistles and thorns and you won't see fruit.

To gain victory over Satan we must come out from under the curse by affirming that man does not live by bread alone—by natural laws—but by every word that comes out of the mouth of God.

Selflessness Instead of Pride

The devil's next attack against Christ consists of an appeal to human pride.

> Then the devil took him to the holy city and had him stand on the highest point of the temple. "If you are the Son of God," he said, "throw yourself down. For it is written: 'He will command his angels concerning you, and they will lift you up in their hands, so that you will

> not strike your foot against a stone.'" Jesus answered him, "It is also written: 'Do not put the Lord your God to the test'" (Matt. 4:5-7).

The second temptation has to do with our fellowship with God, with our holiness and with not tempting Him with our vain manner of thinking. If we paraphrase Satan's appeal here, adapting it to our time, he would be saying something like this: "Use your power in Christ to be admired, to get rich, to manipulate people, to act independently. After all, you are holy. In fact, you are great! Christ will keep you, the angels are at your service. What are you worried about?"

But Jesus kept Himself at the center of the Father's will, instead of making Himself the center. He yielded Himself and served the Father and others in humility, in love, in self-denial, even unto death. He exemplified supremely what the book of Revelation says of the martyrs: "They overcame [Satan, the accuser] by the blood of the Lamb and by the word of their testimony; they did not love their lives so much as to shrink from death" (Rev. 12:11).

We are victorious warriors only when we truly learn to deny ourselves for the love of the gospel and when our testimony is a testimony of faith and praise to God instead of a testimony of complaints and selfishness. We can be anointed for spiritual warfare only when we understand that the power to overcome lies not in ourselves, even in our own self-sacrifice, but in the sacrifice of Jesus, in His blood that was poured out for many (a theme that will be developed in the next chapter).

Resistance to the devil is preceded by submission to Christ: "Submit yourselves, then, to God. Resist the devil, and he will flee from you" (Jas. 4:7).

Jesus knew that the authority that was flowing and moving through Him came from the same essence as the Father, because of His intimate fellowship with Him. Being with His Father was what satisfied His soul, nourished his bones and filled him with peace. Yet He denied Himself this luxury. He "did not consider equality with God something to be grasped, but made himself nothing," becoming a man among men (Phil. 2:6,7).

Often we feel out of sorts when we are surrounded by unconverted people for a long period of time. We desire to speak with someone who speaks our language, the language of the Spirit; we look for Christian people to be able to talk with them. But think of Jesus' situation as He was confronted by Satan in the desert. He had nobody with whom to speak. Yet it was in His self-denial that He found the power to rely on the Father through the Spirit to resist Satan's temptations in the flesh. It is on this reliance that His victorious life is based. He demonstrated that "He who sent me is reliable" (John 8:26).

Because Jesus yielded to the will of the Father instead of living a self-centered life, the devil could not touch Him in the slightest. Surely Jesus could have built up a personal reputation by tending to the thousands of needs He saw during His ministry; but He focused only on what he heard from the Father: "I do nothing on my own but speak just what the Father has taught me" (v. 28).

A multitude of people were gathered at the pool of Bethesda, waiting for the angel to descend and stir the waters; however, Jesus only healed one paralytic (see John 5:1-8).

When people came to tell Him that his friend Lazarus was sick, Jesus could have immediately set out to raise Lazarus and ride the crest of popular attention that was focused on the incident. Instead, He calmly waited for two days, seeking God's purpose and being attentive to the Father's direction.

It is sad to see so many people so caught up with worldly things that they do not have the time to listen to God's voice. It is much easier to go to the pastor and tell him to pray for direction in one's life than to kneel in persistent prayer until we ourselves are allowed to enter the most holy place and, being face-to-face with God, hear His perfect will. But this requires disciplining the flesh, being committed to and in love with the Lord Himself and submitting ourselves to His will.

This is where true victory lies: in listening to Him!

Resisting the devil requires powerful determination. One day several years ago, the Lord showed me how easily we let ourselves be carried along by every difficulty the devil thinks of sending into our lives. The problem stems from our not being totally fed up with the enemy of our souls. When the Holy Spirit put this in my heart for the first time, I reacted and told Him: "How am I not already showing that I am fed up with Satan, Lord? I already don't tolerate anything he does to me."

The Lord answered, "Certainly you do not tolerate him—that is true—but you are not *fed up.* To be fed up with Satan leads to spiritual violence of such magnitude that you declare war on your oppressor, war unto death. You are *determined to overcome, cost what it may.*" You see, I had not been so fed up with the devil that I was willing to declare all-out war against him and to accept the radical changes in my life that a declaration of war requires.

Jesus said, "From the days of John the Baptist until now the kingdom of heaven suffers violence, and violent men take it by force" (Matt. 11:12, *NASB*).

That day I understood the principle that has given me the greatest victories over the devil. I became filled with spiritual violence, or holy anger, so to speak. I drew a line against the devil and made up my mind to forcefully conquer him wherever I encountered him. From that day the devil was informed that if he dared to get involved with me, I was going to trample him with all the strength of God's Spirit, I was going to send him to the divine tribunal for judgment on the slightest thing he did to me, I was going to beat him with the Word of God and with the blood of the Lamb, I was going to use the whole army of angels that Christ had put at my disposal to make war on him and to finish him off! I was no longer going to spend my nights disturbed by Satan's opposition. I was going to sleep deeply, give praise to God and entrust myself into His arms. From that day on, Satan was the one in trouble.

Patience is a fruit of the Spirit. Therefore, the devil does not have patience. And when he sees you determined to do battle with him instead of believing his lies, it causes damage to his kingdom; and he will flee from you with impatience, more quickly than you can imagine.

Worship as Warfare

The third temptation aimed at Christ in the wilderness has to do with worship.

> Again, the devil took him to a very high mountain and showed him all the kingdoms of the world and their splendor. "All this I will give you," he said, "if you will bow down and worship me." Jesus said to him, "Away from me, Satan! For it is written: 'Worship the Lord your God, and serve him only.'" Then the devil left him, and angels came and attended him (Matt. 4:8-11).

Focusing on the worship of God draws our attention away from the human tendency to crave greatness in this world, from the desire to be seen and honored by men, from the search for recognition.

So many people suffer terribly when they are not praised for what they have done. They spend their lives searching for titles conferred on them by the world and even by the Church. They obtain their identity and self-worth from this recognition. But in this they leave themselves vulnerable to demonic humiliation and are continually defeated by the devil, because this world's glory is like a flower, here today and gone the next.

In contrast, Jesus clearly established the foundation of His strength and victory when He said, "Worship the Lord your God, and serve him only" (Matt. 4:10).

Praise and worship to God are among the most powerful weapons in spiritual battle. Psalm 34 is one of the passages which has most ministered to me and allowed me to see great miracles throughout my Christian walk. King David wrote this psalm during one of the most difficult moments in his life. He was all alone and was being pursued by Saul, who wanted to kill him. Abimelech, king of the Philistines, had previously helped David but now had turned his back on him and made him leave. David's wives were kidnapped, and he did not have any food. The situation could not have been more discouraging for the young David.

But in the midst of his distressed situation, David wrote:

> I will extol the LORD at all times; his praise will always be on my lips. My soul will boast in the LORD; let the afflicted hear and rejoice. Glorify the LORD with me; let us exalt his name together. I sought the LORD, and he answered me; he delivered me from all my fears. Those who look to him are radiant; their faces are never covered with shame. This poor man called, and the LORD heard him; he saved

> him out of all his troubles. The angel of the LORD encamps around those who fear him, and he delivers them. Taste and see that the LORD is good; blessed is the man who takes refuge in him. Fear the LORD, you his saints, for those who fear him lack nothing. The lions may grow weak and hungry, but those who seek the LORD lack no good thing (Ps. 34:1-10).

What kept David steadfast and strong in the face of any circumstance? The ability to worship and praise God, knowing that his security was in the Lord and that his God was strong and powerful, a God who heard him, a God who fought his battles and kept him safe from his enemies, a God who was his refuge and strong tower, sheltering him in times of tribulation.

David had learned to stop looking at circumstances and to lift up his spirit in God's presence. He had learned to see and to praise God's greatness, no matter how big the problem. He knew that "the Lord is close to the brokenhearted and saves those who are crushed in spirit. A righteous man may have many troubles, but the Lord delivers him from them all" (Ps. 34:18,19).

Just over a year after my conversion, I was making a living by exporting works of art by Mexican artists to the United States. An American art merchant came and bought some pieces and put me in charge of the whole transaction until the art objects arrived at their destination. One day this American acquired a precious sculpture made out of the finest black marble, weighing about half a ton and valued at approximately $10,000.

At that time I was living in an old apartment on the fourth floor of a building that had no elevator. When the movers brought me the huge marble piece, they could not get it past the second floor, no matter how hard they tried. I decided to have them leave it on one of the landings. It was a Saturday, and I could do nothing until the customs office opened on Monday. But since the odds of the sculpture being stolen were truly impossible, I rested without worry.

On Sunday I went to church; and when I returned, to my surprise, the sculpture was gone. I felt as though the ground had opened up beneath my feet. Not even by selling all I had would I be able to pay for the missing work. I went to my room and fell down before God. He was all I had to rely on.

I started to praise and worship Him, and said, "Thank You, Lord, for this marvelous opportunity to see heaven opened and Your army of angels work on my behalf. Thank You for the privilege of seeing Your power in such a great way. I ask You, Lord, that the sculpture might burn the hands of the thieves and that they will return it in repentance." Then I continued in praise. Later, back at church, I spoke to the pastor about the situation and asked for support in the prayer meeting.

Forty-eight hours later the sculpture appeared intact on the landing. The Lord brought to light who the thieves were: two Americans and a Mexican. They were arrested and taken to prison where we were able to share the love of Christ with them.

I wrote letters of forgiveness, absolving the thieves of all blame. Two of them decided they didn't need Christ, but the other fell to the floor crying out for forgiveness and receiving Christ into his heart. I don't know what happened with the prison records, but the one who received Christ was set totally free, while the other two were deported from the country to be summoned for sentencing to an American prison.

I learned a great lesson: Instead of worrying, praise God all the time. Our Savior and Redeemer lives!

Psalm 149 speaks of the incredible power of praise to undo the devil's power:

> Praise the LORD. Sing to the LORD a new song, his praise in the assembly of the saints. Let them praise his name with dancing and make music to him with tambourine and harp. May the praise of God be in their mouths and a double-edged sword in their hands, to inflict vengeance on the nations and punishment on the peoples, to bind their kings with fetters, their nobles with shackles of iron, to carry out the sentence written against them. This is the glory of all his saints. Praise the LORD (vv. 1,3,6-9).

When we praise God, we are fighting a powerful battle. When we lift our hands, they are like swords lifted up in worship but having the spiritual power to injure the enemy. Here is the spiritual meaning of David's statement that "he trains my hands for battle" (Ps. 18:34). Our God receives such worship when, instead of falling like victims and being oppressed by circumstances, we lift up a new song, praising Him from the innermost parts of our being and exalting Him for His greatness, power and strength.

Living in the Power of the Spirit

Luke's Gospel provides this conclusion of the account of Christ's temptation:

> When the devil had finished all this tempting, he left him until an opportune time. Jesus returned to Galilee *in the power of the Spirit*, and news about him spread through the whole countryside (Luke 4:13,14, emphasis added).

The anointing for victory in spiritual battle comes when we are submitted to God, when we resist the devil and when we make a categorical determination of the position we want him to have in our lives.

We will never have authority over any demon who is attacking someone else until we have defeated the devil in our own lives. For this reason we see churches that are weak, without any authority and full of misfortune and defeated people. Too many Christians in such churches have never made a definite determination to overcome the devil. They have never made the decision to grasp hold of God's power. They look only to the banks for answers to their financial problems and only to medical practitioners for the solution to physical problems.

The great men and women in the history of Christianity are those who once made an irrevocable, unbreakable decision: to take up their position seated with Christ in the heavenly places and never to give away their place of authority to the enemy of their souls.

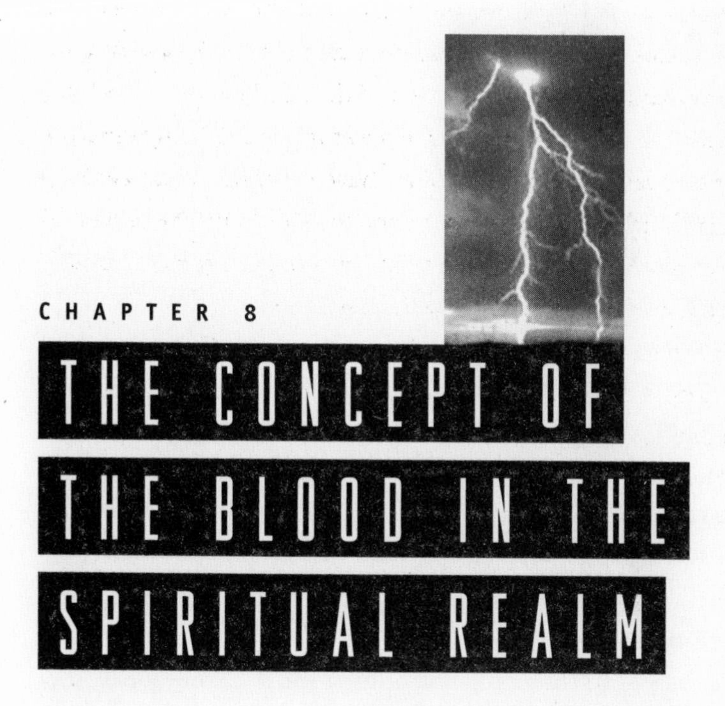

CHAPTER 8

THE CONCEPT OF THE BLOOD IN THE SPIRITUAL REALM

In my ministry to Christians, I have found that many people do not appreciate the significance of the blood in the spiritual realm.

The blood is the first atoning ingredient that God revealed to man. From the fall of mankind to the revelation of the glorious future of the Church, God has constantly intervened in history for the salvation of man. Salvation through the blood is a golden thread woven through all of Scripture. It is an ever-flowing river of life. Therefore, we will never have peace of spirit and total victory over sin and Satan without understanding the powerful mystery of the blood.

Blood in the Story of Salvation

In the epistle to the Hebrews, referring to the Tabernacle in the wilderness, the writer asserts that "Only the high priest entered the inner room, and that only once a year, and never without blood, which he offered for himself and for the sins the people had committed in ignorance" (9:7).

Since man fell into sin in the Garden of Eden, he has found himself separated from God. The wages of sin is death, the basic meaning of which is "separation"; and the only way to overcome this separation and to draw near again to the Creator is through the sacrifice of an animal. This victim takes the place of the sinner, and one life is taken so the other can prevail.

Abel was the first priest and the first prophet to whom God revealed the power of the blood. Abel's life was consecrated to offer sacrifices to the Lord. The only purpose of the flocks Abel tended was to provide burnt offerings to God, since man only started to eat meat after the flood (see Gen. 9:3). Since then and up until now, blood has been the only way of drawing near to God.

Man cannot receive God's blessings, fellowship, revelation or power apart from this precious element that was the first statute ordained to provide sinful man a way to draw near to a holy God.

Without sacrificial blood, Enoch would never have been caught up into heaven, nor would Noah have found favor with God. After the flood, Noah offered up to God the sacrifice of a burnt offering, sanctifying the earth for the Lord with the blood (see Gen. 8:20). And after the cleansed earth had been consecrated to the Lord, His first commandment to man was: "You must not eat meat that has its lifeblood still in it. And for your lifeblood I will surely demand an accounting" (Gen. 9:4,5).

In this commandment we see that blood is something which belongs to God and therefore cannot be taken lightly. God designed the blood with a holy principle deep within it and placed His seal on it. It must, therefore, be treated with respect.

This principle of the blood is repeated with Abraham and Isaac, through whom God formed His chosen people, a people that would give birth to the Messiah. God now added a new concept to sacrifice: the submission of the heart, complete surrender to God. When Abraham showed that he was willing to offer to God his own beloved son, Isaac, he showed that he was actually giving himself to God. And Isaac, lying on the altar before God substituted the ram caught in the nearby bush, became a type of Christ by being willing to give up his lifeblood.

The principle of sacrifice in the story of salvation is that one life is given to save another life. This is the principle of every sacrifice ordained in Scripture. It is the principle of atonement and of the redemption with which Christ bought us. We see this repeated in the Passover. God told Moses:

> On that same night I will pass through Egypt and strike down every firstborn—both men and animals—and I will bring judgment on all the gods of Egypt. I am the LORD. The blood will be a sign for you on the houses where you are; and when I see the blood, I will pass over you. No destructive plague will touch you when I strike Egypt (Exod. 12:12,13).

Here God is establishing a foundation that would continue in perpetuity: Those who are under the protection of the blood of the sacrifice cannot be touched by death.

It was not only necessary to kill the paschal lamb and pour out its blood; the people had to put the blood on the door frames of their houses. Likewise, it is not enough that Jesus spilled His blood; it has to be put on the doors of our hearts, which are our spiritual houses.

Jesus promises, "Here I am! I stand at the door and knock. If anyone hears my voice and opens *the door*, I will come in and eat with him, and he with me" (Rev. 3:20, emphasis added). This door of the heart is the inner part of a human being, and the meal Christ refers to is the supper of the New Covenant in His blood.

Here God is dealing with man again through the blood, but this time in a more direct way than at Sinai. In the New Covenant, He is going to establish His thoughts, His righteousness and His law in the hearts of His people.

Still, the events at Sinai contained the same principle in action:

> And he sent young Israelite men, who offered burnt offerings and sacrificed peace offerings of oxen to the Lord. And Moses took half of the blood and put it in basins, and half of the blood he dashed against the altar. Then he took the Book of the Covenant and read in the hearing of the people; and they said, All that the Lord has said we will do, and we will be obedient. And Moses took the [remaining half of the] blood and sprinkled it on the people, and said, Behold the blood of the covenant which the Lord has made with you in accordance with all these words. Then Moses, Aaron, Nadab, and Abihu, and sev-

> enty of the elders of Israel went up [the mountainside]. And they saw the God of Israel [that is, a convincing manifestation of His presence], and under His feet it was like pavement of bright sapphire stone, like the very heavens in clearness (Exod. 24:5-10, *AMP*).

The blood of the sacrifice brings with it the presence, the manifestation and the revelation of the living God.

The Significance of Blood

Why did God choose blood? Perhaps we associate blood with some accident we have suffered. But the blood in God's plan has a far deeper meaning.

The Life Is in the Blood

Blood is man's vital fluid, containing life itself: "For the life of a creature is in the blood, and I have given it to you to make atonement for yourselves on the altar; it is the blood that makes atonement for one's life" (Lev.17:11).

Because the life is in the blood, the value of the blood has to do with the level of life that it represents. For example, the blood of a person is more valuable than that of an animal; and the blood of Christ is beyond all expressible value.

The blood of Jesus contains all of the life of God—eternal life. When He instituted the Lord's Supper, Jesus said:

> I tell you the truth, unless you eat the flesh of the Son of Man and drink his blood, you have no life in you.

> Whoever eats my flesh and drinks my blood has eternal life, and I will raise him up at the last day. For my flesh is real food and my blood is real drink. Whoever eats my flesh and drinks my blood remains in me, and I in him (John 6:53-56).

To drink the wine of Communion implies the appropriation of everything Christ's blood represents. It is the very essence of His magnificence. It is both the life force drained from Him at the crucifixion and the blood that flowed again through His resurrected body. It is also the greatest revelation of His love for men. All the power against the devil is in the blood. The blood is the door through which we enter to be united with God. It is where the Spirit of God and the spirit of man merge. For these reasons, the wine of the Supper is the real drink that strengthens the spirit.

Many churches speak little of the blood, and many congregations seldom sing songs that mention the blood. Some denominations have even eliminated the blood altogether. This is a tragic omission, since the blood of Jesus is the way through which we can approach the throne of grace. He could have never been the Way (see John 14:6) if He had not poured out His blood, because it is the blood that has atoning value when it is offered on the altar.

The Blood of the Sacrifice

The Old Testament describes the significance of the blood of sacrifice:

> [Moses] then presented the bull for the sin offering, and Aaron and his sons laid their hands on its head. Moses slaughtered the bull and took some of the blood, and with his finger he put it on all the horns of the altar to

> purify the altar. He poured out the rest of the blood at the base of the altar. So he consecrated it to make atonement for it (Lev. 8:14,15).

Putting their hands on the head of the animal that was going to be sacrificed, in this case the bull, had the purpose of identification. It identified the animal as a sacrifice in which the life, or the blood, of the victim took the place of the priest's life.

In an even more significant way, the blood of Christ was the sacrifice of His life for ours. Christ was "the Lamb that was slain from the creation of the world" (Rev. 13:8). This speaks of how Jesus spiritually took the place of the sacrificial lamb, even before God had created the world. In His absolute foreknowledge, He knew that man would fall into sin; so even before creating him, God gave Himself for man's redemption.

The Spirit of God portrayed as "Wisdom" in Proverbs 8:30,31 says, referring to the times before the creation of the universe, that "I was the craftsman at [Jesus'] side . . . rejoicing in his whole world and delighting in mankind." This is evidence that before the world came into being, God's entire plan of redemption was already conceived. Everything was created and made, existing first within God Himself and then in the visible world. "By him all things were created" (Col. 1:16).

When the Holy Spirit came upon the virgin Mary and the power of the Almighty covered her with His shadow, Jesus' spirit already slain (since the foundation of the world) fused with the egg in Mary's womb. From His birth, His blood spoke to Him, leading Him to this sacrifice.

During His earthly life, His blood continually brought every desire of self-satisfaction to death. Even before the cross, the sacrificial blood that ran through Jesus' veins continually led Him to self-denial and giving Himself for others.

From childhood, each time He sat down at the Passover table year after year, He must have come to see in a different light one of the four symbolic cups of this celebration being filled with wine and lifted up as a representation of the longed-for redemption of man. He saw the day when this cup would no longer be only a hope but a reality—the cup He would take in His hands to establish the New Covenant in His own blood: "This cup is the new covenant in my blood, which is poured out for you" (Luke 22:20). And His blood never stops speaking to him of this moment when He would give His life for humanity. I imagine that every time Jesus entered the Temple, He would stop in front of the bronze altar where the sacrifices were offered and think, *One day I will be that lamb on the altar.*

Remaining in the Blood

The blood of Jesus continues to function today in the lives that have been redeemed by His blood. Unfortunately, however, a large majority of Christians never receive all the power and unbreachable armor available to them in the blood of Jesus, because they have never entered into it.

Victory over Satan requires entering into and remaining in the blood of Jesus. At the first Passover, the Jews had to remain inside their houses where the blood had been placed. In the same way, Jesus said, "Whoever lives in Me and I in Him bears much (abundant) fruit. However, apart from Me [cut off from vital union with Me] you can do nothing" (John 15:5, *AMP*).

When Jesus established His New Covenant at the Last Supper, He said, "This cup is the new covenant *in* my blood" (Luke 22:20, emphasis added). He did not say *of* my blood or *by* my blood but *in* my blood. You do not enter into the blood of Jesus by just mentioning that someone is covered with the blood while he or she is actually squandering his or her life in darkness.

The blood receives its authentic power and has effect when we come in true repentance to the Cross and remain there, because the Cross is the only place the blood of Jesus was poured out for us. The apostle John wrote:

> This is the message we have heard from him and declare to you: God is light; in him there is no darkness at all. If we claim to have fellowship with him yet walk in the darkness, we lie and do not live by the truth. *But if we walk in the light*, as he is in the light, we have fellowship one with another, and the blood of Jesus, his Son, purifies us from all sin (1 John 1:5-7, emphasis added).

It is in His blood, in His life, in His light, that the power of God cleanses us, renews us, trains us and clothes us with all His authority. Again from John: "Whoever eats my flesh and drinks my blood remains in me, and I in him" (John 6:56).

The life of the Almighty produces the life of Jesus in us. Sin put an end to the plan God had for intimate communion with man. Sin separated God from that which He loved the most. Sin destroyed unto death the beloved of God. For this reason the Lord hates sin, because it isolates us completely from His presence and from his intimacy.

God had to provide something strong enough to counteract all that sin had destroyed, something so powerful that it would satisfy His anger and the cry for justice, which the price of sin demands.

Only one thing could have this power: the love of God welling up from the eternal fountain of redemption through the blood of His Son. Only one thing could rip the veil in the Temple that was interposed between man and God: the blood of Jesus poured out for the sins of the world. The blood of Jesus is that "blood of the eternal covenant [that] brought back from the dead our Lord Jesus, that great Shepherd of the sheep" (Heb. 13:20).

The Power in the Blood

The blood of the covenant overcame death and opened the tomb! The blood of the covenant opened the heavens; the blood of the covenant defeated the kingdom of darkness forever; the blood of the covenant is one of our most powerful weapons in warfare.

The devil cannot stand the proclamation of the blood. No demon can resist one who is anointed by the Holy Spirit and proclaims the power in the blood. All of Satan's army was present at the crucifixion. All the demons attended the prince of darkness' defeat, when he was overcome by the blood. All the satanic hosts were there when the act that stood against us was nailed to the Cross, disarming and making a public spectacle of the powers and authorities (see Col. 2:13-15). They all concocted the plan to do the worst to Jesus that could be done to any human being, but they all failed.

Fellow believer, you have to know that demons do not have children. Every demon who wants to affect your life was defeated at the Cross, and you have the authority to remind them of that fact. You have the power to bring to their remembrance how the satanic kingdom was destroyed through the blood of the Lamb. Every time you mention the blood of Jesus, the Father is glorified, the Son is exalted and the power of the Spirit is released.

There is a power that shakes the foundations of hell! There is a power that makes the demons believe and tremble; there is a power that establishes the kingdom of God and disarms the devil; there is a power that releases the power of the Almighty, opens the heavens and manifests the glory of God.

That power is the blood of Jesus Christ, the Son of the Living God, who is King of kings and Lord of lords. To enter into the blood of the New Covenant is to enter into the torrential outburst of the very life of God, which, like a brilliant flame of divine light, scatters the darkness.

They who know what it is to enter into the blood of Christ will never be overcome!

PART TWO

TERRITORIAL WARFARE

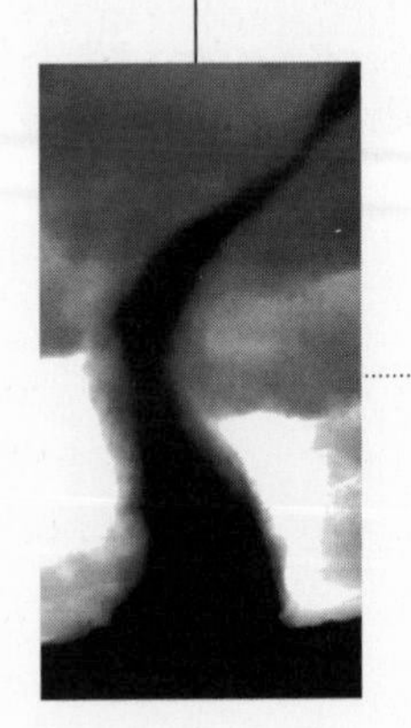

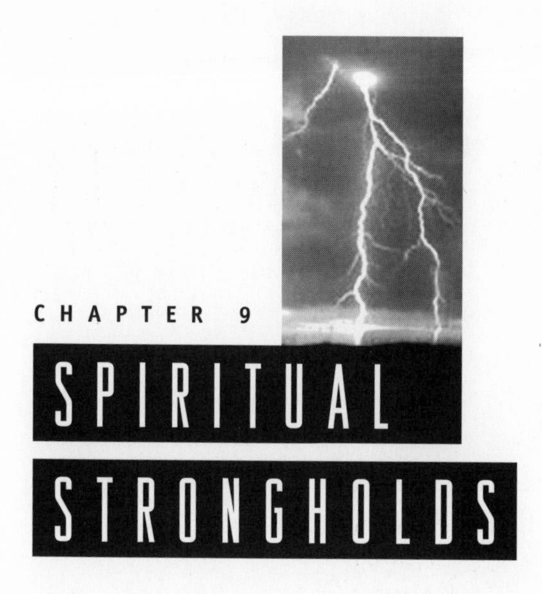

CHAPTER 9
SPIRITUAL STRONGHOLDS

Much of the emphasis on spiritual warfare in the last few years has been in the area of defending the mind as the primary battlefield. We have learned the importance of holding our position in Christ against the devil's attacks. Now, however, God is calling us to change our emphasis in at least two fundamental ways.

First, we as the Body of Christ need to move from the defensive to the offensive and reclaim from the enemy everything he has stolen from us over the centuries. And second, we must understand that our battlefield extends beyond the personal into *the territorial*—into the realm of territories, nations and cities.

Through the teaching of Dr. Rony Chaves, we have learned that the city is the basic concept for understanding territorial battle. Dr. Chaves holds:

The city is a structure of government, a hold in a developed society. It represents a place of political, religious and social influence; and it is in the cities where important decisions are made. Unlike a village, a city has within its limits a much greater complexity in all its organization, development and infrastructure.

The city is the most complete symbol for representing the Kingdom of God in the Bible. We see this in the glorious heavenly city, described by the apostle John in Revelation. This city, "The New Jerusalem," speaks to us of the great eternal reign of God with man. We have to realize that each part of it, its walls, its gates, its towers, its foundations and everything that is in it are symbols which represent the Supreme King of the universe in His majestic Kingdom.

God showed himself to David as a castle, a strong tower, as a fortified wall and all these structures are attributes of the great strongholds in cities in days gone by. It is essentially important to know a city in all its aspects with great precision because this is what opens the panorama for us to understand the large range of concepts in the spiritual realm.

Cities represent the seat of a throne, dominion or specific government. In the old days they would put walls and ramparts around their cities to fortify them and keep them from their enemies.[1]

Every great general, every conqueror, knows that in order to take a kingdom it is necessary to enter the city, do away with the previous government and establish a new one.

An attacking army can win all the battles in the field, but as long as it does not take the city, the enemy government will prevail. In order for the children of Israel to possess the Promised Land, Joshua had to penetrate the stronghold of Jericho. God gave him the strategy, and the walls fell down. Only then could the Israelites destroy the enemy's government—only when they had taken the city, which was the seat of the opposing power. Taking cities was the necessary tactic for conquering the land of Canaan. This is important for really understanding the spiritual reality behind the bloody wars of the conquest period under Joshua in Israel's history.

Now knowing the effectiveness of this strategy, it is essential for us to comprehend how Satan, being only an imitator of God, has taken ownership of this concept to build his own kingdom and how building strongholds in the spiritual realm is the way he governs nations, cities, towns and districts.

Foundations of the Stronghold

How and with what does the devil build? In the natural world, the first thing one does in building anything is to prepare the ground and lay the foundation. This same principle is equally applicable in the spiritual realm.

To form a clearer view of this process, let's take a little look at the early development of mankind after the expulsion of Adam and Eve from the garden. Thanks to his longevity, man started to multiply rapidly and fill the earth. But he was no longer man in union with his creator. He was now fallen, enslaved by Satan. Because of this, evil began to increase at the same rate as man's numerical growth and soon reached abominable extremes.

Although the Word has left us few recorded facts, those which have been preserved, along with those that tradition has gathered, fill us with dread. Even the fallen angels, whom Scripture calls the "sons of God" in Genesis, dared to marry the women of Earth in terrible acts of sexual depravity (see Gen. 6:1,2). From this inbreeding sprang a race of giants known as the "Nephilim" (6:4), the "descendants of Anak" (Num. 13:33).

Immediately after this reference to the Nephilim, the Bible says that the world had come to such a depraved state that God "was grieved that he had made man on the earth" (Gen. 6:6) and He determined to destroy the human race. To do so, He sent the great flood and allowed only Noah and his family to be saved.

After this cataclysm, the earth became repopulated through these survivors. Unfortunately, the seed of evil was still sown deep within man's heart. Noah's son Ham, who had inherited more wickedness than the others, made fun of his father and vexed him because of Noah's unintentional nakedness. In turn, his father, Noah, cursed one of Ham's sons—Canaan. From that branch, in the course of time, a strong man called Nimrod was born—a man who became a symbol of evil for all time.

The Scriptures tell us that Nimrod was a "mighty warrior" and a "mighty hunter" (Gen. 10:8,9). Neither the name Nimrod nor the phrase "mighty hunter" have been well understood. The basic meaning of Nimrod is "rebel"; and according to ancient Jewish tradition he is the man who raised his fist in anger, in challenge to the Lord. Nimrod established cities in Shinar (see 10:10), which became a center representing man's pride and arrogance against God:

> As men moved eastward, they found a plain in Shinar and settled there. They said to each other, "Come, let's make bricks and bake them thoroughly." They used brick

> instead of stone, and tar for mortar. Then they said, "Come, let us build ourselves a city, with a tower that reaches to the heavens, so that we may make a name for ourselves and not be scattered over the face of the whole earth" (Gen. 11:2-4).

This city, Babylon, is the origin of the whole idolatrous system of the devil, the cradle of all false religions, idolatry, occultism and all the current philosophies that influence our civilization for evil today.

Tower of Evil

The Tower of Babel (see Gen. 11:9) in Babylon is a physical reflection of what Satan had built in the spiritual realm through the abominations of men. Stone, which was usually used for construction, symbolizes that which comes from God, while the man-made brick symbolizes the desire to replace what comes from God with what man has created. In the spiritual realm, brick and tar symbolize the work of sin that man gives to the devil as a building material.

Nimrod, full of the satanic mind-set, wanted to establish the idea in this world that man can reach heaven through his own deeds. Through him, Satan established his control of the fortress, because there was already a stronghold in the spiritual realm that the devil used to rule all the inhabited earth. The Tower of Babel was, therefore, the visible manifestation in the natural world of the stronghold the devil had built.

To this day, the world is filled with such towers of evil—strongholds in the heavenlies—reflected on Earth as cities filled with corruption, principalities, powers and rulers of darkness. As a result, millions of human beings are controlled like puppets.

City and Mountain of God

Although the devil has established strongholds that seem indestructible to the human mind, Christ came to establish the City of God on the earth. This city is the most powerful structure in the whole universe, because it's founded on Jesus Christ and is built up, not with man-made bricks, but from living building blocks—men and women filled with the Spirit of God.

This is the city built on a high mountain, Mount Zion. Mountains are a symbol of kingdoms, and they are among Satan's favorite places to set up his governments and structures. But Scripture says that a holy mountain is being manifested, a mountain that will flatten every high mountain of Satan: "In the last days the mountain of the LORD's temple will be established as chief among the mountains; it will be raised above the hills, and all nations will stream to it" (Isa. 2:2).

We must leave behind our childish fears and see the truth: Satan is not in control; God is in control! Satan has built strongholds over all the earth, but the time has come for the mountain of God to be gloriously raised up above every other mountain. It is time for the Church to take up its position of authority and to tell every mountain to "be cast into the sea" (Mark 11:23, *NKJV*). The mountains will have to fall and the governments of the devil will have to fall, because a glorious Church is being raised up. There are men and women of God clothed in a power so great that they are pulling down satanic strongholds, decreeing like Zerubbabel: "What are you, O mighty mountain? Before Zerubbabel you will become level ground" (Zech. 4:7).

Scripture says of the Lord: "On that day his feet will stand on the Mount of Olives, . . . and the Mount of Olives will be split in two" (Zech. 14:4). God is raising up prophets, warriors of God who know that the feet of the Lord crush the mountains, crumble the kingdoms of the devil. We are seeing the fulfillment of what the Lord told Joshua: "I will give you every place where you set your foot, as I promised Moses" (Josh. 1:3).

There does not exist a human foot with a sole that can undo the devil's government and give us the earth for Christ. Only the holiness from the sole of the foot of Jesus Christ expressed through His servant can make His enemies a footstool.

The Lord is working through His disciples. Their soles are being used to trample the mountains–satanic strongholds; they have so completely denied themselves of self that nothing of them remains. The torrent of God's life and power can flow only through the feet of those who practice such humility and self-denial.

Brothers and sisters: Never stop being willing for something great to happen in your life, because God is raising up prophets with the feet of Christ–men and women who will not only make the heavens tremble but the earth as well!

Note

1. Dr. Rony Chaves, Mexicans in Victory conference, April 1994.

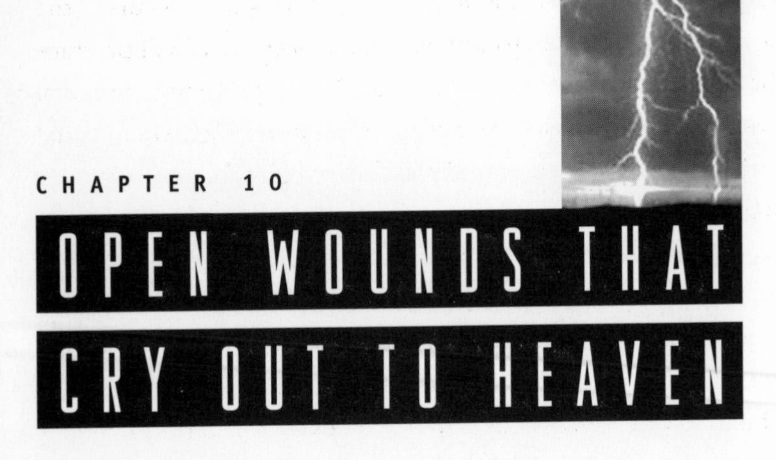

CHAPTER 10

OPEN WOUNDS THAT CRY OUT TO HEAVEN

In the previous chapter, we noted that Satan strongly desires to harm the earth, because it is in this way that he lays the foundation of his strongholds. In this chapter, we will take a look at how Satan carries out this shameful task.

God first made man in His image and likeness. He breathed the divine Spirit into man and placed him in a garden full of the splendor of His glory. The beauty of Eden was intimately related to Adam's original spiritual condition, reflecting God's government over both the animate and inanimate creation. The apostle Paul could, therefore, write that "since the creation of the world God's invisible qualities—his eternal power and divine nature—have been clearly seen, being understood from what has been made" (Rom. 1:20).

The Curse of Sin

Genesis 3 records the tragic account not only of the fall of man but of creation as well. Because man fell into sin, God cursed the earth: "Cursed is the ground because of you. . . . It will produce thorns and thistles for you" (Gen. 3:17,18). By cursing the earth, God allowed the devil to have the dominion, the keys and the authority over the earth. All this had originally been given to man; but in this, the most despicable act of treason, man gave this glorious gift of God over to Satan.

From this we see that there is an intimate relationship between man's spiritual condition and the condition of the earth. In this connection, the term "earth" refers not only to the land, which now produces thorns and thistles, but also to the inhabitants and social structures that make up the nations of the earth. Since the Fall, therefore, the devil's governance has been apparent in the spiritual, social and physical realms of the earth.

Satan hates everything God created, and it is his goal to destroy it. In our own era we can see that in the natural realm the greatest expansion of evil on the earth is reflected in the expansion of pollution and the ravages of what the world calls natural disasters. Paul describes the scene graphically, in terms of an earth that "groans":

> The creation waits in eager expectation for the sons of God to be revealed. For the creation was subjected to

> frustration, not by its own choice, but by the will of the one who subjected it, in hope that the creation itself will be liberated from its bondage to decay and brought into the glorious freedom of the children of God. We know that the whole creation has been groaning as in the pains of childbirth right up to the present time (Rom. 8:19-22).

In wounding the earth through tempting man to sin, Satan began to lay the foundation for his strongholds. As John Dawson writes, the devil works "through the guilt and hurts that people have not been delivered from."[1]

The physical consequences of both sin and obedience are clearly expressed in Moses' farewell speech in Deuteronomy. On the one hand:

> If you fully obey the LORD your God . . . You will be blessed in the city and blessed in the country. The fruit of your womb will be blessed, and the crops of your land and the young of your livestock. . . . Your basket and your kneading trough will be blessed (Deut. 28:1,3-5).

On the other hand:

> If you do not obey the LORD your God . . . You will be cursed in the city and cursed in the country. Your basket and your kneading trough will be cursed. The fruit of your womb will be cursed, and the crops of your land, and the calves of your herds and the lambs of your flocks (vv. 15-18).

Sin brings plagues to a nation. It brings famines, epidemics and wars. These problems, bad enough in and of themselves, are made worse when man tries to resolve them by submitting himself to satanic forces. Destructive behavior and violence increase when people search for answers in magic, the occult, witchcraft and idolatry. This whole cycle, orchestrated by the devil, strengthens his kingdom and makes his strongholds more and more powerful.

> "Woe to the obstinate children," declares the LORD, "to those who carry out plans that are not mine, forming an alliance, but not by my Spirit, heaping sin upon sin; who go down to Egypt without consulting me; who look for help to Pharaoh's protection, to Egypt's shade for refuge" (Isa. 30:1,2).

And Habakkuk 2:12 tells us: "Woe to him who builds a city with bloodshed and establishes a town by crime!"

Satanic power finds opportunistic access to inflict his havoc on the earth in two basic ways: idolatry (intimately tied in with witchcraft) and injustice.

Idolatrous acts are designed to obtain supernatural advantage from so-called gods. People desperate for help or greedy for power become allies with cruel gods and enter into deep places of slavery that can only be broken by the atonement of Christ. Again from John Dawson: "Injustice opens the door for demonic oppression, an oppression that people are powerless to deal with outside of the cleansing, healing grace of God."[2]

In the Bible we see this with clarity during the reign of Ahab and his wife, Jezebel. Their abominations brought a drought that lasted for more than three years. The demonic activity through the priests of Baal was so alluring that the people swayed between two allegiances. There was terrible confusion over whether Jehovah or Baal was the true God. The earth was wounded by the sins of the people, as God withheld the rains until the prophet Elijah exposed the false gods by defeating their priests (see 1 Kings 18).

Accursed Lands in Our Time

Today we see how the land and its people have been terribly cursed in those countries where there is a high level of satanic activity. Here are some examples:

- India, a country where more than 3,000 gods are worshiped, is immersed in absolute poverty. People die of hunger in the streets.
- In Africa, many parts of which were the cradle for voodoo magic, terrible plagues and diseases such as AIDS have ravaged the population, along with extreme poverty.
- People are suffering in the former Soviet Union. For years the government testified against God; now the Russian people are being disabled by demonic powers, as a new tyranny arises that brings with it extortion, crime and shortages.
- Haiti is a country that has been directly offered to Satan. In the central square of Port au Prince there is a statue of a black pig with a plaque that reads, "This nation belongs to Satan." Haiti is inundated with horrible diseases, and hunger and poverty are found on every street.
- The United States, a country born with the Bible in its hand and blessed by God as the world's leading power,

is filled with curses, too. The land is wounded by sins—3 million abortions each year, legal rights for satanic churches, occultic music and television programs, recreational drugs and every form of abuse. Suicide and murder plague the nation's young people.

- The occult is rampant in Mexico, a country founded under ancestral covenants. Syncretism has allowed the powers of darkness to infiltrate parts of the Catholic church in Latin America through the assimilation of local pagan rites and practices; Catholics from other countries are often horrified by the abominations they see in some of the Mexican churches. Meanwhile, Santeria (Caribbean witchcraft) ceremonies are openly performed on television, while Christian stations are prohibited. The government has long been infested with corruption; and millions cry out for justice in this nation plagued by poverty, sickness, pollution, murder and robbery.

Dr. Rony Chaves said in 1992 that God had revealed that there was an enormous demonic stronghold over Mexico City. It was an ancient castle with thick walls, filled with dirt, cobwebs and squalor. A gigantic, black, winged power was seated in the castle chambers, almost filling one room. Its presence was terrible and its power extended over a great part of the continent. It was revealed in this prophetic encounter that wounded, horrible demons from different Latin American countries came to this stronghold. There they were received by this satanic power, healed and then sent out again with even more power to their cities. (See chapter 17 for an account of our counterattack in Mexico.)

If this power is over the skies of Mexico, it is an indicator of the condition of our inhabitants. It is the root from which comes the evil, violence, corruption and all the very real tragedies that we experience.

Covenants with Satan

It is important to define the origins of the satanic stronghold on Mexico, where its foundations are and what God's strategy is for tearing it down. The principles which the Holy Spirit has taught us are not only useful for Mexico but for other countries as well.

In the previous chapter, we mentioned that man's sinful actions are what give the devil material with which to build. From the fact that all truth is parallel, we can arrive at interesting conclusions if we view individuals as the basic units that make up a society. As we shall see, we are still suffering from pacts that our ancestors made with demonic forces long ago.

Man is essentially a spirit that lives inside a body and communicates with the outside world through the soul. Likewise, a nation is a "spirit" which is established in a territory (its "body") and which expresses itself to the outside world through the personality of its people (its "soul").

In the same way a human's soul is affected by hurts, violent impacts, rejection and occult and idolatrous practices and covenants, the soul of a people, for lack of a better expression, also receives the same impacts from such practices, bringing damage and demonic oppression over the land.

We see this truth in the Bible when God refers to Israel or one of her tribes as if it were a person bound by evil or hurting: "The guilt of Ephraim is stored up, his sins are kept on record" (Hos. 13:12). And again He declares, "The LORD will call [Israel] back as if [Israel] were a wife deserted and distressed in spirit–a wife who married young, only to be rejected. . . . O afflicted city, lashed by storms and not comforted" (Isa. 54:6,11).

God also describes the restoration of Israel in personal terms: "'In that day,' declares the LORD, 'I will gather the lame; I will assemble the exiles and those I have brought to grief. I will make the lame a remnant, those driven away a strong nation'" (Mic. 4:6,7).

Throughout history some nations have been so hurt by social injustice and marred by horrible crimes of racism that many were driven to the point of extinction by indescribable acts of genocide. Nations are hurt by tyranny and by corrupt governments headed by people who are in covenant with the devil. Such acts result in nations actually being wounded by the hand of God, as He wounded Israel so long ago.

If we analyze the history of our Latin American countries, we can conclude that their current woeful condition is due to the ties, pacts and terrible wounds that our people have suffered since ancient times. In Mexico our ancestors made covenants with pagan gods. These pacts have not been broken and in fact are still being given life by indigenous and esoteric sects that perform ceremonies at which blood is shed by witches and sorcerers. It is more and more important every day to know these things so we can fight effectively against the powers of darkness.

All this evil prevails while God's people don't act, while we don't come to a full awareness of the spiritual condition of our cities and countries. I strongly believe that today the Holy Spirit is trying to awaken us to the profound truths that critically affect our countries. There is among us unconfessed sin and sinful covenants and oaths that have not been broken. Ancestral doors that were opened to invite foreign gods to take possession of our land have not been closed. The power of blood sacrifices that have not been canceled by the atoning blood of Jesus Christ continues to give the devil the legal right to work in our nations.

"Remember this, fix it in mind, take it to heart, you rebels. Remember the former things, those of long ago" (Isa. 46:8,9).

Evil Rooted in History

To rid the land of such evil, it is of fundamental importance that we analyze a city's history from its foundation. Just as the time of gestation of a fetus in its mother's womb and the first years of life determine the development of a person, so the principles upon which a city is built determine its later development. Just as the soul of a child can be profoundly marked by circumstances that occur while it is in the womb, so the spiritual foundations which will govern a city are forged when it is established.

Several books could be written about the injustice and the demonic pacts in the history of Mexico, but that is not my intention. It is enough to say that today our land is hurting because of incredible abuses committed throughout our history. As John Dawson writes:

> The greatest wounds in human history, the greatest injustices, have not happened through the acts of some individual perpetrator, rather through the institutions, systems, philosophies, cultures, religions and governments of mankind. Because of this, we, as individuals, are tempted to absolve ourselves of all individual responsibility.[3]

We must face up to the fact that the state of any nation is affected by sins of both the individual in particular and the nation as a whole. Usually, when we reflect on our sins and failures as human beings, we become so individualistic that it is as if only our own personal relationship with God is important. It is the personal fault of others if they do not reach the Promised Land. Their lukewarmness and worldly lifestyles are the only factors at fault. We envision ourselves as some kind of benefactor, giving to the world the wonderful things God has given us; and if people refuse them, it is their own doing.

Certainly the prayers of individuals who honestly seek God can have an effect on the lost. But the Spirit wants to open our eyes and lead us to understand that not only individuals but cities and nations are also bound by Satan's chains. We all bear some of the guilt. And if we do not confess these sins at the family level, at the group level, at the local level and even at the national level, identifying ourselves with God as His true priests, these sins will continue to bring death. They will increase in the body politic just as wounds that have never healed spread their infection in the individual's body.

For example, the indigenous races of the Americas have been violently hurt, enslaved and humiliated by the Spanish and Portuguese conquistadors. Hatred for these crimes continues to flow through the veins of both natives and mestizos. Racial sins that have not been confessed, as well as sins of arrogance that stem from a spirit of pride, racism and superiority, continue to take root in the hearts of Creoles and mestizos.

This damages the soul of a nation. It brings demonic oppression over entire populations, because the historic sins still bind us and because we are too wrapped up in ourselves to put aside individual concerns in favor of interceding as a people on behalf of our nations.

That which was decreed for Israel in prophecy is also true for the peoples of the American continents. Here is my adaptation of the prophecy given to Isaiah (1:3-7, *AMP*):

> The ox [instinctively] knows his owner, and the donkey his master's crib, but America does not know or recognize Me [as Lord], My people do not consider or understand. Ah, sinful nation, a people loaded with iniquity, offspring of evildoers, sons who deal corruptly! They have forsaken the Lord; they have despised and shown contempt and provoked the Holy One of Israel to anger; they have become utterly estranged (alienated). Why should you be stricken and punished anymore [since it brings no correction]? You will revolt more and more. The whole head is sick, and the whole heart is faint (feeble, sick and nauseated). From the sole of the foot even to the head there is no soundness or health in [the nation's body]—but wounds and bruises and fresh and bleeding stripes; they have not been pressed out and closed up or bound up or softened with oil. [No one has troubled to seek a remedy.] [Because of your detestable disobedience] your country lies desolate, your cities are burned with fire; your land—strangers devour it in your very presence, and it is desolate, as overthrown by aliens.

Restoring the Glory

Some sins embrace entire cities, cursing our lands and impeding God's Holy Spirit from coming over certain sectors. A fundamental principle in removing this curse and bringing revival is restoring God's glory over a place: When glory comes, and power falls, the devil and his hosts are subdued, the veil falls and souls run to the feet of Christ. But the glory will not come unless we apply the structure designed by God to bring it about. This structure consists of the following:

1. Identification (identifying with the sin to intercede for those in its grip)
2. Confession
3. Reconciliation
4. Restitution
5. Spiritual battle
6. Worshiping God

In order to be able to overcome the forces of hell, it is essential that the kingdom of God be brought to the places in bondage to Satan. It is necessary to pour out the oil of glory that reaches and touches hearts. It is essential to raise up a church so full of the Spirit that the demons and gates of hades cannot prevail.

The devil has established his principalities and powers for one main reason: because the glory of God has not been established in that place.

In too many places, instead of God's glory there are deep wounds. Too often, the first Europeans brought a distorted gospel to the land. There was no dialogue and no respect for indigenous people. They were simply considered to be of the devil and were whipped and beaten and submitted to torture to make them receive an unknown God. Many died without even knowing what was happening. Although they were people made in the image of God, they were treated and killed as demonic beasts who had no rights or free wills.

Today we want to talk of freedom and love, but the blood that was previously shed still speaks. The Scripture says that the blood of Abel and the blood of Christ still speak (see Heb. 12:24). So also does the blood of thousands of First Nations people speak, saying "I am full of pain from past injustice."

Today we want to speak of unity within the Body of Christ, but we are full of racial divisions and guilty of not addressing and healing past wrongs. From generation to generation, great acts of deep scorn exist between races; nationalistic attitudes are rooted in pastors and ecclesiastical leaders that often express themselves in hatred toward anything that comes from abroad. All this evil continues, because the blood of so many from the past is crying out "This injustice has not been healed!" The devil seizes this opportunity to divide churches and deprive the Body of Christ of blessings. As long as there is no identification, no confession, no reconciliation, no restitution, no spiritual battle and no worship among believers, there will be areas in the hearts of God's children that will continue to be governed by the devil!

Horrendous ancestral sins divide families, too. The conquests in the New World were accompanied by the rape of women, the destruction of many homes and the slaying of Indians–all killed by the lustful desires of Iberian soldiers. This destruction planted the thirst for revenge among Mexican and other Latin people. Unable to bear any more abuse, the oppressed peoples in the Mexican Revolution and similar uprisings in South America committed vengeful massacres of Spanish families and Creoles. Possessions were burned and people were hung in front of their families; many women were raped. The conquerors were stripped of everything. Why this terrible violence? How did it occur? It's because centuries of pain remained unhealed. There were wounds in the people that were rooted as far back as when gold and riches of the Americas were carried away to Europe by the ton.

This ongoing hatred and destruction is like a long, continuous prison sentence that includes no possibility of release. Each thinks, *I have the right to steal because my fathers were plundered! I have the right to humiliate any Spaniard, white or foreigner I come face-to-face with because the Spanish insulted us! And vice versa: I have the right to humiliate any Mestizo I come across, because the revolutionaries took the lands from my fathers.* The same situation often occurs in the United States between Native Americans and the descendants of European settlers and also between whites and blacks.

Perhaps it is hard for some to accept this assertion that such harsh attitudes persist today. However, they are subconsciously rooted in our attitudes. They are unhealed hurts that have become swollen and bleeding sores. The infection has to come out, because it is building up pressure within the wound and causing much pain. God is calling us to clean the wound, to remove the infection and to salve it with the oil of the Spirit by the process of identification, confession, reconciliation, restitution, spiritual battle and worship.

Our races come bearing generational marks: rejection, fear of authority, rebellion, independence, loneliness, isolation, fear of compromise, melancholy, inferiority, terrible addictions. This comes from the fear of facing a reality they cannot resolve in their own strength.

For these reasons the earth is cursed and sick. The land cannot be healed by the repentance and devotional life of isolated individuals. Corporate sins, those committed by people groups, must be dealt with at the corporate level by identifying ourselves with and including ourselves in a specific category of human beings and asking forgiveness for the sins of the nation or group.

Daniel was not a man given over to sin. Far from it; he lived a life of service to God. But the Lord showed him that his personal intercession for the nation of Israel was the key for delivering it from captivity and slavery. To intercede is to identify with the sinner, to put oneself in the sinner's place, to stand between God and the transgressor. Of course, this is effective in the spiritual realm only if those who repent on behalf of their nations have in humility already confessed their own sins (see

Jas. 5:16). Otherwise, this identificational repentance is being done in presumption.

The revealing of God's glory in the healing of the wounds of the world awaits such confession, followed by fervent, effectual prayer for races and nations.

Notes

1. John Dawson, *Healing America's Wounds* (Ventura, CA: Regal Books, 1994), pp. 53, 54.
2. Ibid., p. 56.
3. Ibid., p. 30.

CHAPTER 11

THE ORGANIZATION OF GOD'S ARMY

It is significant that the apostle Paul uses military terminology when speaking of standing against Satan and his forces. It is nothing less than "warfare" (2 Cor. 10:4, *NKJV*). When we speak in military terms, we do well to understand some fundamental concepts regarding the structure of an army, how it is coordinated and the role of each soldier.

I have been blessed by God in this area, in that my grandfather was one of the great generals of the Mexican Revolution. As a young girl, I heard him tell stories about the war, stories of battles or of the military prowess of great leaders in our history. As we have said, all truth is parallel—as things are in the natural world, so are they in the spiritual realm. Following this principle, what can we learn about the army God uses in spiritual warfare?

The Role of Prayer Warriors

For years we have been mobilizing the Church to pray, since prayer is the most powerful way for God's supernatural intervention to be manifested in changing the course of human events. We see the Holy Spirit leading us into a more precise type of prayer and causing each prayer warrior to find his or her correct place. Because of this, prayer warriors are making incredible strides and are destroying the devil's strongholds as never before.

We said at the beginning of this book that together with the outpouring of the Holy Spirit, which brings the prophetic mantle, a glorious awakening of God's army is coming. As never before we are seeing prayer groups, spiritual warfare squads and massive meetings of intercession being raised up. The spiritual battle that is upon us is stirring hundreds of Christian writers, leaders and preachers.

Amazing revelation is being given to those who are taking up the challenge of combating the forces of hell until they are subdued. It is as though a wave of divine wisdom is revealing the marvelous secrets of God that have been set aside for the last days. It has been prophesied that scientific advancements will increase during the last centuries; and together with this monumental development that we are seeing in the natural world, the knowledge of God will continue to be opened up in a glorious way in the spiritual realm.

While meditating upon the progressive work of restoration that is being done by the Holy Spirit, I observed how God is more and more putting His enemies under the feet of Christ, just as Hebrews 2:8 says: "[God] put everything under his feet. In putting everything under him [Jesus], God left nothing that is not subject to him. Yet at present we do not see everything subject to him." The writer goes on to say that Jesus "sat down at the right hand of God. Since that time he waits for his enemies to be made his footstool" (Heb. 10:12,13).

These verses clearly show that the spiritual battle, the subjection of the devil's empire to the kingdom of God, is a process being carried on throughout time. Although Jesus completely finished the work of redemption on the cross of Calvary, He gives us the privilege of being part of His great victory, clothing us in His power so we can take the whole satanic army captive. Truly "his intent was that now, through the church, the manifold wisdom of God should be made known to the rulers and authorities in the heavenly realms" (Eph. 3:10).

Praying and doing spiritual battle have to be a work led by the Holy Spirit. We must not enter the spiritual world in a casual way and without direction. Dr. C. Peter Wagner tells of two missionaries who, against the advice of local Christian natives, decided to cut down a tree at which different kinds of satanic ceremonies took place. Both were struck dead on the spot.[1]

This should impress upon us how dangerous it is to occupy a position of battle for which we have not been trained. In any army there are positions that require rigorous training and deep internal preparation. Although we should not glorify or overstate the power of the devil, who is no more than a defeated foe, neither should we underestimate his astuteness or capacity for battle. Recognizing our human weakness, let us in humility come into a place of complete dependency on God. Although the power of Satan is limited, he is without any doubt the master of deceit and evil.

It is written that in the last times evil will multiply upon the face of the earth, and there will come a weakening of faith that will cause some, even among the chosen, to be deceived. Jesus asked, "When the Son of Man comes, will he find faith on the earth?" (Luke 18:8). Without a doubt, Satan is attacking with all he has in these last days. This is one of the primary reasons why it is so important to define the functions of an army and the strategies for each battle.

The Generals in the Battle

God is equipping modern-day prophets for the role of directing spiritual warfare, just as generals in the natural realm are equipped to direct armies. The ministry and mantle of the prophet are indispensable in coordinating the spiritual army and revealing God's strategy for the battle. This ministerial office and that of the apostles form God's covering for His army. They lead, guide and protect the army, in wisdom defining the strategies of attack and the right timing to carry them out.

In order to fully comprehend what the Holy Spirit wants to do and when He wants to do it, we need to have vision and understanding. Imagine facing an enemy stronghold with a whole army trained for war; then a group of gullible soldiers, because of simple enthusiasm, decide prematurely that now is the time to attack. If "now" is the moment that the enemy is best prepared and on guard, the small squad would certainly be defeated. On the other hand, if God revealed through His prophets the moment when the stronghold is weak, with many of its troops away on another mission, the enemy fortress could be easily taken and victory guaranteed.

The prophetic ministry, with its officers and intelligence corps, can discern the timing and strategies of the supreme general–Jesus Christ.

The Intelligence Corps

God's intelligence corps consists of His spies, who examine history and are aware of all the attacks the devil wants to undertake.

Soldiers in the divine intelligence corps are up-to-date with the latest news in the mass media. They analyze maps and discover the places where the devil has established what we call pillars of iniquity–places of intense sinful activity within the population. These are the soldiers who do the spiritual mapping.

The Commandos

Among the officers are squads of commandos–Green Berets, as they are called in some countries. These are highly specialized soldiers who launch specific missions to take strongholds. Their main task is to bind and tear down the strongman or strongmen who control a city.

God's commandos are ministers with prophetic characteristics; they are effective intercessors who are gifted with great courage to confront principalities and powers face-to-face. They move in key places shown to them by the Holy Spirit and, like the prophets of the Old Testament, obey the voice of God, even to the point of death and no matter how ridiculous the divine order may seem. (I will refer to this in more detail later.) These groups include soldiers who are in major deliverance ministries.

The Artillery Brigade

God's army includes a brigade that is in charge of weapons of massive attack. In the natural world, the light artillery consists of grenadiers and those who carry the cannons, machine guns, etc. In the spiritual world, these are ministers of praise, groups of tambourine players that encourage the fighters and ministers of war dances.

The heavy artillery in the natural world is made up of armored tanks, submarines and bombers. In God's army, the artillery consists of intercessors with a prophetic anointing who groan in the Spirit with such power that their prayers are true bombs. Within these ranks we will see caravans of cars that surround cities with intercession and prayer walks (see chapter 17). This strategy is used to pull down spiritual walls of iniquity in a territory and to mark the boundaries of areas that are being taken for Christ.

Prayer vigils also make up part of the artillery corps, since it is through powerful prayer that God weakens strongholds that His people are trying to capture. It is utterly important to consider these troops in the execution of a strategy against the forces of Satan.

The Infantry

An army's infantry consists of the foot soldiers. In some armies they are armed with bayonets and rifles. These are the soldiers charged with making the actual advance on a city. In the case of a highly protected stronghold, they enter into action once the commandos have captured the strongman and the gates to the city have been pulled down either by the commandos or heavy artillery. They also make up a defensive corps that besieges fortified cities.

In God's army, these are the people who fight hand-to-hand, so to speak. It is the evangelistic action and the work of personal deliverance that snatches souls one by one from the devil.

This brief description of an army could be described in far more detail. The point is that we must understand the diversity of positions that make up an army and the important part that each type of warrior plays in the success of a war. Even those we would consider the least significant can have great revelation and spiritual power, and in the past some of them have stood out as great heroes in battle.

Note

1. C. Peter Wagner and F. Douglas Pennoyer, eds., *Wrestling with Dark Angels* (Ventura, CA: Regal Books, 1990), p. 87.

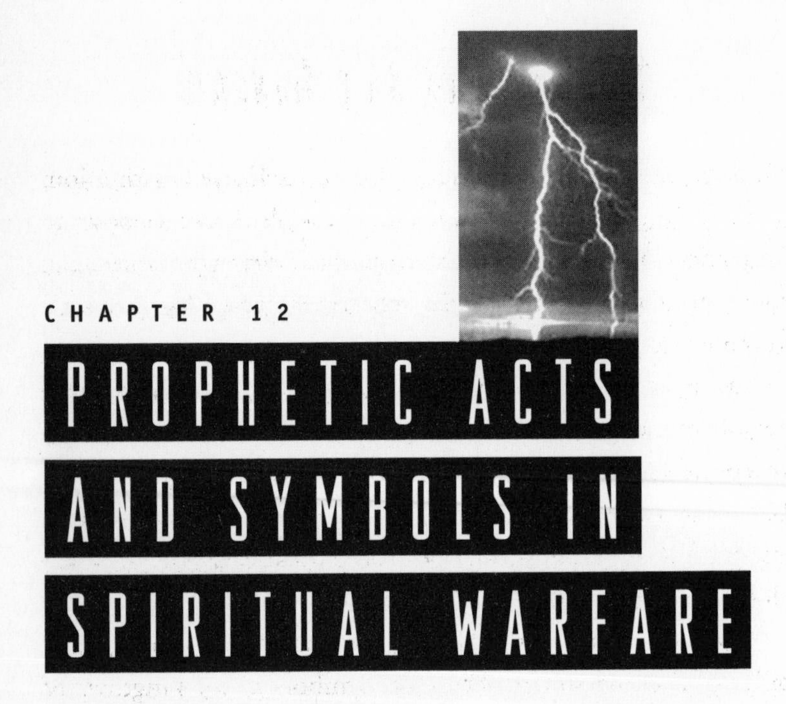

CHAPTER 12

PROPHETIC ACTS AND SYMBOLS IN SPIRITUAL WARFARE

One of the things we see that God is restoring within the prophetic movement is the use of symbols and prophetic acts. God is speaking to us in specific and clear ways through His Word to bring about victories and important advances both in spiritual battle and the establishment of His kingdom.

We can see how symbols are used by examining the Scripture verses that God is showing to many of His prophets. I consider it extremely important to make a clear study of this theme so as not to fall into grave error through lack of knowledge. We need to understand the use and meaning of symbols. This enables us to flow with God's Spirit and to not fall into the trap of wrongly handling these symbols, as do the occultists.

Symbols of the Divine

Throughout history God has revealed Himself and His kingdom to us through symbols, figures and models. From Genesis to Revelation, the Bible is full of symbolism through which God shows us His personality, His redeeming work, His heavenly kingdom and all that He is, as well as how He relates to man.

Without making an extensive list, we see, for example, the person of Christ revealed in many ways, from the door to the sheepfold (see John 10:7) to the rock in the desert (see 1 Cor. 10:4), the Tabernacle (see Heb. 9:1-11) and the bronze serpent (see John 3:14). From the simple to the most complex, these are all symbols which speak to us of Christ.

We see symbols of the Holy Spirit, such as rivers of water, a pillar of fire and smoke. There are symbols of the kingdom of God, such as a flock, a city and a banquet. The people of Israel are portrayed as a fig tree or an unfaithful wife; and the Church is symbolized as a bride and as a building made of living stones. And just as is the case in Scripture, an ever increasing number of symbols are appearing on the scene today to serve in the advancement of revelation.

It is important to know that while a symbol may be of divine origin and have nothing inherently wrong in it, we must take care to apply it correctly. Symbols are used widely in both the Old and the New Testaments. A symbol is something of earthly origin that links the spiritual world with the natural realm. Many times God moves through them to loose His power and truth to us and the surrounding world.

For example, God told Moses to lift up a bronze serpent in the desert so that everyone who looked at it could be healed (see Num. 21:9). Through this symbol, to which Christ is later compared (see John 3:14), God took the sin and sickness of the people upon Himself and released divine healing.

Elisha told Naaman to bathe seven times in the Jordan River to be healed of leprosy (see 2 Kings 5). The river in and of itself did not have healing powers, but it was an important symbol of how obedience to the spoken word of the prophet God would release His healing power. In addition to bathing's symbolizing the washing away of sin and disease, the number seven symbolized the completion of the word of wisdom God gave to Elisha. The creation of the world also was completed in seven days.

At the bitter waters of Marah, Moses threw a branch of a tree into the water, and it was made sweet (see Exod. 15). What better way to symbolize the sweetening power of Christ in redeeming us from the bitter waters of sin? In the New Testament we have baptism in water, a symbol of renewal of the spirit and cleansing. The waters are not magic and have no inherent power; it is God who moves through this act of obedience and destroys through baptism the power of sin in our lives (see 1 Pet. 3:21).

We are commanded to anoint the sick with oil (see Jas. 5:14,15). The oil in and of itself does not have any power; but the Holy Spirit, symbolized by the oil, works through this act of obedience. In a similar way, partaking of the elements of the Lord's Supper, which are only bread and wine, symbolize the body and blood of Christ; and the one loaf of bread points to the unity of the Church.

Although God often simply manifests Himself through the spoken word, on many other occasions He uses symbols to do so. When we analyze the prophetic books of the Bible, we find an enormous number of prophecies that were decreed through the symbolic acts of God's prophets.

God commanded Ezekiel to make a model of the city of Jerusalem and to lie beside it for 430 days to represent the fact that the prophet was bearing the sins of the people (see Ezek. 4:1-8). Later He told Ezekiel to put a pot on the fire until the rust (or scum) was consumed and to prophesy over it (see 24:1-12).

God commanded Isaiah to walk around barefoot and naked for three years (see Isa. 20:2-3). He ordered Jeremiah to bury a linen belt until it was rotted (see Jer. 13:1-11) and to put stones on brick pavement at Pharaoh's palace in Tahpanhes to indicate an invasion by Nebuchadnezzar (see Jer. 43:8-11).

God commanded Elisha to throw salt in a spring of water, so it could be healed (see 2 Kings 2:19-22). And Gideon was commanded to hide torches in jars of clay and then to break them, in conquering the city of Jericho (see Judg. 7).

One could make an unending list of the symbolic instructions God has given throughout history. What is certain is in every instance God could have released the power of His word through His servants without physical symbols, and His prophetic word would have come true just the same. But in the mystery of His infinite wisdom, He often chooses to accompany His word with symbols.

Why does He do this? Perhaps the answer is that God uses symbols to dramatize or emphasize something. Perhaps it is to enlarge our faith or to bring glory to His name when the vessels He uses are obedient to His Word. Perhaps it is simply because God is sovereign and can choose to work in whatever way He wishes.

Strategic Battle Symbols

On some occasions God has told us and many other prophetic ministers to use physical symbols, especially in strategies of territorial battle. I recall an occasion when I did not know how to find the faith to pray for one of the church's sheep who was sick with cancer. This happened at the beginning of my ministry when I did not yet have the spiritual maturity God has blessed me with by His grace over the years.

The woman was in pain, because her children had not yet come to Christ; and she did not want to go to be with the Lord without having her house in order. One afternoon while I was fervently praying, I clearly heard the voice of the Holy Spirit speak "Isaiah 38:21" to me. I excitedly opened the Bible to see what this verse says and when I read it, I was astounded. It says, "Isaiah had said, 'Prepare a poultice of figs and apply it to the boil, and he will recover.'" I did not understand anything at that moment, but a strong conviction caused me to get up out of my chair and go to the market to buy some figs. I was not surprised when they told me that fig season was extremely short and they had only one basket of figs left.

I arrived at the home of my beloved sister in the Lord, Marce, and told her all about the word I had received. The two of us believed it with all our heart. So I started to peel the figs and mash them. The pulp was a rosy color, just as if I was putting my hands in raw flesh. At this moment I felt as though I was sinking my hands into the very wounds of Jesus, while the Holy Spirit reminded me of the passage in Isaiah 53:5: "But he was pierced for our transgressions, he was crushed for our iniquities; the punishment that brought us peace was upon him, and by his wounds we are healed."

I knew that the figs themselves had no healing power, but I believed that they were a symbol of the wounds Jesus suffered for us and that God would move through this symbol. I simply obeyed the instruction of the Holy Spirit and applied the figs to the woman. And it worked. Her lesions, which had reached her bones, began to close up and her pain diminished. God used this miracle to lengthen her life enough for her to be able to put her house in order. During this time many people from all over came to visit her, and she testified of Christ's love to them all. Her life and her testimony left fruit that today is a solid and established church. I did not have the faith that was necessary for this miracle, but the symbol loosed my faith and with it the power of God.

In Paul's teaching about the gifts of the Spirit, the Word says there are different kinds of working (see 1 Cor. 12:4-6). I understand this to be a supernatural move of the Holy Spirit that is demonstrated in a specific moment where God is working in a given circumstance. We frequently see this while doing spiritual battle.

When we speak of strategies of war and symbolism used on the spiritual battlefield, the Spirit's most used gifts are the gift of prophecy, the word of knowledge and the word of wisdom. Through these means, God has worked wonders.

With the gift of knowledge, He has shown us the exact places where sacrifices have been made, bewitched homes that are keys to delivering a place, structures of strongholds and places where strongmen are seated. The gift of knowledge allows us to know in a supernatural way something that is happening or something that occurred in the past. The word of wisdom guides us in knowing how to take a stronghold, how the Lord is going to move, what symbols He is going to use, if any, and how to use them. The gift of prophecy releases the decrees and the power of God to win the battle.

Symbols False and True

When speaking of prophetic symbolism and instructions given by the Holy Spirit, something which is strange to the natural mind, some may wonder if we are falling into occultism by using symbols.

Throughout my Christian walk, I have seen so many snares of the devil used on the servants of God that I have become extremely discerning of which moves are of Satan and which are of the Holy Spirit. First, I think it is always important to be discerning before lashing out in criticism and judgment of good works. God may be doing something which is difficult for the natural mind to understand, but that does not automatically make it something from the devil.

It is important to discern not with the mind but with the *spirit*. We should not turn our noses up at something that somebody says is of God, nor deny it in such a way that we negate the move of the Holy Spirit, or even worse, blaspheme the Holy Spirit.

On analyzing these themes in great depth, I have discovered another reason why God allowed me to reach the depths of occultism before turning to Him. In magic, freemasonry and all forms of occultism, symbols, objects and proclamations of faith are used effectively to produce powers of darkness. In this, Satan is showing that he is imitating the way God produces *light*; Satan is not a creator but an imitator, wanting to beguile us into believing that he is God.

Therefore Satan, the master of deceit, looks for every possible way to resemble the Most High, especially when dealing with those attributes that unmistakably belong to God. I am referring to worship and to God's miracle-working power. In too many cases people bow down to idols not because they have horns and a tail. but because they appear as heavenly beings coming from God himself. People look for healing and divine favor in idols, and the devil often gives it to them. In fact, to people who would rather be deceived than to know the truth, God actually "sends them a powerful delusion so that they will believe the lie" (2 Thess. 2:11).

Satan is obvious when he comes stealing, killing and destroying; but he is incredibly deceitful when he tries to imitate God. In this area, the dividing line between truth and falsehood is extremely subtle. It is like a counterfeit bill. The devil would never try to pass off play money as real. He would use monetary paper and, where possible, the original engraver's plates, leaving the serial number as the only error. The principle of deceit is that what it produces is incredibly similar to that which is genuine.

Satan disguises himself as an angel of light, because there are angels of light in heaven. He performs false signs and wonders, because there are real signs and wonders. What we must not do is eliminate everything divine just because the devil tries to copy it. The devil receives praise from pagan worshipers, but we are not going to stop praising God because of it. Although the devil foretells and prognosticates, God continues to speak prophetically to His people. The devil twists the Word of God, but we are not going to stop reading and using the Word.

Since symbols are used by God in both the Old and New Testaments and are also used by the devil himself, the question is how to tell the difference between those used by God and those used by Satan.

When a Symbol Is Used by God

1. An object never has any power of its own; the power is in the Holy Spirit, not the object. Jesus did not walk around with His bag of mud, healing the blind; nor did Isaiah travel with his fig poultice, curing boils.
2. God sovereignly allows the anointing of the Spirit to remain on some of the objects His servants used as symbols. This was the case with Elijah's mantle (see 2 Kings 2:8,13,14) and articles that had touched Paul

(see Acts 19:11-12), although it was not the case with all the mantles or garments of the apostles. God decides when, what and how such symbols bear His Spirit. On occasions God has allowed His servants to pray over the clothes of some sick person who could not be easily moved, and in such cases the anointed clothes are the only point of contact to release faith. It is faith and the anointed Word proclaimed by the servant of God that unleashes the miracle, not the piece of fabric.

3. It does not matter if the object or symbol is removed from the place where God first used it or if it is washed. It is the power of God through His Spirit, not the object itself, that exercises influence. On some occasions God has taken us to anoint some places that inevitably have to be cleaned as part of a daily maintenance program. This will never eliminate what the Spirit of God has released through objects in that place.
4. Every symbol used must have biblical support.

When a Symbol Is Used by Satan

1. The object itself may have diabolical power.
2. The sorcerer is the one who decides when and how it is used–in accordance with magical formulas and traditions.
3. The object remains impregnated with unclean spirits and continues to have influence as long as it remains in the appointed place.

If we clearly understand these points, we will avoid many mistakes. The problem I have seen has been when we try to generalize an instruction God has given for a particular instance.

Merely because a symbol works in one case does not mean it is to be used in every similar case.

For example, Paul told Timothy to drink a little wine for his bad stomach. This doesn't mean that every time someone has gastrointestinal problems they should take a drink of wine. To fall into making symbols generalized objects of power without listening in each case to the voice of God is to fall into witchcraft.

Similarly, God is revealing extraordinary methods and powerful strategies in spiritual warfare. However, what works in one city or in one country won't necessarily work in another. Our responsibility is to fall to our knees and to listen to what God, who is Lord and Supreme General of His army, wants to do. He is King, not us. Let's walk with prudence, courage and under the anointing and the fear of God.

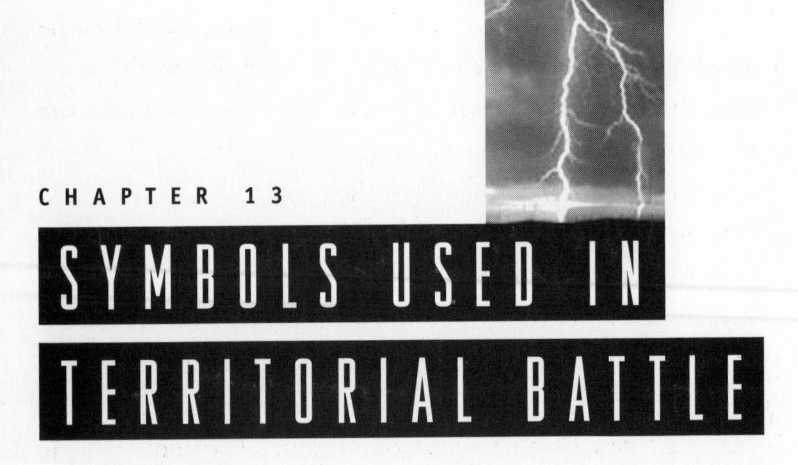

CHAPTER 13
SYMBOLS USED IN TERRITORIAL BATTLE

Regarding the symbols that God is revealing to many warriors in territorial battle, I want it to be clear that I do not desire to make a doctrine out of this or intend to impose my views on anyone. This is simply personal revelation that I believe God has given to us to conquer territories, cities and countries.

On every occasion these symbols have been employed, we have seen a powerful move of God. My desire is to share what God has given us with those of you who are fiercely fighting for your nation so that our experience may be of use to you.

Anointing with Oil

Oil is a symbol of the Holy Spirit and of His anointing poured out. This symbol is perhaps the most commonly used for consecrating a place and for releasing the presence of the Holy Spirit over it.

Consecrating oil was involved when God reaffirmed to the patriarch Jacob that He had given the Promised Land to Israel as an inheritance: "The land I gave to Abraham and Isaac I also give to you, and I will give this land to your descendants after you" (Gen. 35:12). Then God went up from him at the place where he had talked with him. Jacob set up a stone pillar at the place where God had talked with him, and he poured out a drink offering on it; he also poured oil on it (vv. 13,14).

Note that this was long before the giving of the Law, which had its own prescribed use of consecrating oil. Its use apparently came from the gift of the word of wisdom.

Later, the Tabernacle in the wilderness and its utensils and its priests were also anointed with oil, symbolizing that they were set apart for ministry to God (see Lev. 8). Also in Old Testament times, God revealed other universal symbols such as the shedding of sacrificial blood for the atonement of sin. Where did Abel get the knowledge of making sacrifices to Jehovah (see Gen. 4:4)? Where did Jacob get the idea of building altars to God, pouring oil on them and offering drink offerings (see Gen. 35:13,14), long before such symbolic acts were commanded under the Law?

And why does such symbolism reappear in the book of Revelation? "Then I heard what sounded like a voice among the four living creatures, saying, 'a quart of wheat for a day's wages, and three quarts of barley for a day's wages, and do not damage the oil and the wine!'" (Rev. 6:6). No doubt the answer is that

God has ordained these as timeless symbols of His power over forces that would violate the sanctity of His creation.

Several of us once engaged in territorial warfare by attacking the major temple of idolatry in Mexico City (see chapter 17). We completely surrounded the place, pouring out oil as we went and anointing each altar in the name of Jesus. We decreed that this place, where all kinds of witchcraft and idolatry had been performed, would be robbed of its power.

After this spiritual battle, God blessed us with a tremendous earthquake as a sign of victory! Within two weeks, the main priest of the temple appeared on television saying that a sudden crack in the building could not be explained. Engineers came from various countries, and they all concluded that the building would inevitably fall. From this date, the basements that had been places of terrible acts of high magic have remained closed. Glory to God!

The Drink Offering

In this same passage (Gen. 35:13,14), we have seen that Jacob also poured out a drink offering. The drink offering in this passage, according to the *Caribbean Bible Dictionary*, was a small portion of wine that was poured out on the land as a symbol that all the blessings of God would come to the land. Calling this symbolic act a drink offering implies that the priest, or in this case Jacob, first drank of the cup before pouring it out.

Wine is also a symbol of the ratification of covenants. In all Oriental cultures, including Israel's, covenants were sealed with a meal in which one partook of bread and wine in a rite that gave legal status to the covenant. Many of us who are engaged in spiritual warfare have come to the conclusion that lands that have been cursed through pagan and satanic covenants have to be set free from these ties by symbolic acts that cancel corresponding rites performed when the covenants were first established. It is important to break every covenant that has been made over particular places and to replace them by establishing a covenant of God over such places.

What we do is partake of the fruit of the vine, the symbol of the new covenant through the blood of Jesus, and extend over the land the covenant that is over us. On an individual level, Jesus taught that if a person (or personal house) is cleansed of evil spirits but not filled with the Holy Spirit, the person's final condition is worse than it was to begin with (see Matt. 12:43-45). Our work of delivering a place or a land of its evil covenants and replacing them with a new covenant in Jesus' name follows the same principle.

Earlier in this book we noted how the earth's wounds can be healed through identificational repentance. We saw that what is a spiritual principle for an individual also applies to a group of individuals who make up a nation. The basis of this principle is that when a person is delivered, he needs to come to Jesus for his house to remain clean. Likewise, when a land is set free from prior evil covenants and curses that are over it, it is necessary to establish a new covenant with Jesus Christ over the land.

When Joshua entered the land God had promised Israel, the first thing he did was build an altar to God as a symbol of the consecration of the land and establish God's presence in the middle of a territory still dominated by paganism. The question now facing spiritual warriors is how to go about symbolically building altars as a sign that we are conquering the nations God has given into our hands.

The most visible way would be to establish churches in a territory. But if we are going to take a volcano or a State Department, which has been consecrated to the devil, it is doubtful that we would be able to build a church in these places. We can, however, annul demonic activity in such places by building a 12-stone altar and pouring oil and wine over it.

I remember quite an intense moment when we were taking the pyramids of Teotihuacan. I was leading a team to cancel the covenants that had been made in the sacrificial palace, where a great number of human sacrifices had been carried out. As it was still an area of anthropological study, the site was closed to the public. We had started the battle early in the morning, so the place was practically empty. The Holy Spirit compelled me to go inside where the strongman had his seat. I asked the team of warriors to cover me in prayer. Then, asking God to make me invisible, I jumped over the protective fencing and entered the restricted area.

I felt an oppression as a prickling of the scalp. The Holy Spirit comforted me, telling me not to fear because the Lord was going before me with great power. I had to go down into a basement in the dark. In the distance, I felt the presence of a very strong power. I have to admit my knees shook more than once.

When I arrived at the basement, the Lord opened my spiritual eyes; and I could see an enormous winged demon on the seat of sacrifices, like a gigantic vampire, almost filling the whole room. Without hesitating I attacked it, confessing its defeat through the blood of Jesus and decreeing the Word of God with great power.

Then I started to break every covenant that had been made with the devil through the shedding of blood in that place. The hideous power before me was furious, so I wasted no time. I threw oil and wine over it and commanded it to sink into the abyss. In that moment in the spiritual realm, a red whirlpool like fire arose from the depths of the earth and absorbed the demon. A new covenant had been sealed by the blood of Jesus.

Scant seconds after I returned outside and rejoined my group, several soldiers in charge of the security of the place arrived and surrounded the whole site. Glory to God! Satan always arrives too late!

Consecrated Stones

Stones play an important role in territorial warfare. They are a symbol of Christ, "the Rock" (1 Cor. 10:4, *AMP*). Just as when one acquires a plot of land its boundaries may be marked by stones and posts which serve as identifying landmarks, so it is in the spiritual sense.

When such stones are inscribed with Bible passages, they serve a purpose somewhat like the phylacteries with Scripture passages reminding the Israelites that they belonged to God. They were commanded to "tie them as symbols on your hands and bind them on your foreheads. Write them on the door frames of your houses and on your gates" (Deut. 6:8,9).

When we take a city, we write Scripture verses on flat surface stones and place them around all the territory we are going to take, establishing before the devil that this ground now belongs to Christ. We also place stones with verses written on them that decree Satan's defeat in enemy territory, temples of idolatry and sites of witchcraft.

On some occasions God has given us the word of Jeremiah 43:9-13:

> While the Jews are watching, take some large stones with you and bury them in clay in the brick pavement at the

> entrance to Pharaoh's palace in Tahpanhes. Then say to them, "This is what the LORD Almighty, the God of Israel, says: I will send for my servant Nebuchadnezzar king of Babylon, and I will set his throne over these stones I have buried here; he will spread his royal canopy above them. He will come and attack Egypt, bringing death to those destined for death, captivity to those destined for captivity, and the sword to those destined for the sword. He will set fire to the temples of the gods of Egypt; he will burn their temples and take their gods captive. As a shepherd wraps his garment around him, so he will wrap Egypt around himself and depart from there unscathed. There in the temple of the sun in Egypt he will demolish the sacred pillars and will burn down the temples of the gods of Egypt."

Once when we were taking an important stronghold in Mexico City, the Spirit led us to place stones (we placed 12) inside the building and decree this same prophecy, proclaiming that the kingdom of God would spread over them. The following week the city was shaken by 72 earthquakes. As a result, one of the walls of the building crumbled. When this happened in the natural world, we knew that in the spiritual realm a great victory had been gained.

The Use of Salt

After our first great seizure of Mexico City for Christ, I was praying and meditating whether what we had done would have any lasting effects or whether we would have to do it again periodically. As I prayed, I heard the voice of the Spirit say, "Covenant of salt." I looked in the Bible and in several study books for references to salt, and I discovered a number of things.

Salt is a symbol of perpetuity. In 2 Chronicles 13:5, King Abijah of Judah said, "Don't you know that the LORD, the God of Israel, has given the kingship of Israel to David and his descendants forever by a covenant of salt?" By this he meant that the use of the preservative salt seals a covenant forever.

The Old Testament speaks of sealing sacrifices and offerings with salt: "Season all your grain offerings with salt. Do not leave the salt of the covenant of your God out of your grain offerings; add salt to all your offerings" (Lev. 2:13). Although today we do not offer sacrifices in a temple, because this was fulfilled by the New Covenant, I mention it so we can understand the meaning of this symbol and its effect in perpetuating a covenant.

We are living in times of dense darkness over the earth. Covenants with the devil are being made on every side, through witches, satanists, idolatrous processions and invocations of spiritism. Rampant sinfulness implies that entire countries are being given over to demonic spirits. In the face of such acts, we use salt as a substance indicating the superior and perpetual character of the covenants of God that we establish against such moves of the devil.

Salt was also used to bring barrenness to an enemy's land. We read in Judges 9:45: "All that day Abimelech pressed his attack against the city until he had captured it and killed its people. Then he destroyed the city and scattered salt over it."

On the other hand, salt can have a purifying effect, as when Elisha used it to heal the water: "Then he went out to the spring and threw the salt into it, saying, 'This is what the LORD says: "I have healed this water. Never again will it cause death or make the land unproductive.'" And the water has remained wholesome to this day, according to the word Elisha had spoken" (2 Kings 2:21,22).

When we took the volcano of Irazu in Costa Rica, something beautiful happened: We had done everything the Holy Spirit had shown us, and we had finished by scattering salt on the mountain. On the way down, the Lord opened the spiritual eyes of one of the warriors and myself, and we saw how He had surrounded the entire volcano with angels with blazing swords swinging back and forth with great speed.

The Use of Grain

Grain is a symbol of fruit, harvest and revival. We have only used this symbol on mountains, having not felt that we should use it elsewhere. The psalmist said, "May there be abundance of grain in the earth on top of the mountains; its fruit will wave like the cedars of Lebanon; And may those from the city flourish like vegetation of the earth" (Ps. 72:16, *NASB*).

When, in taking a stronghold or city, God leads us to take possession of the mountains that surround it, then we throw the grain from this high place, prophesying the harvest of souls that will come after the battle.

As the understanding of spiritual warfare prospers and the prophetic is more and more accepted by the army of God, we will see many other symbols used. God is using prophetic acts and symbols as very creative and powerful weapons against the enemy.

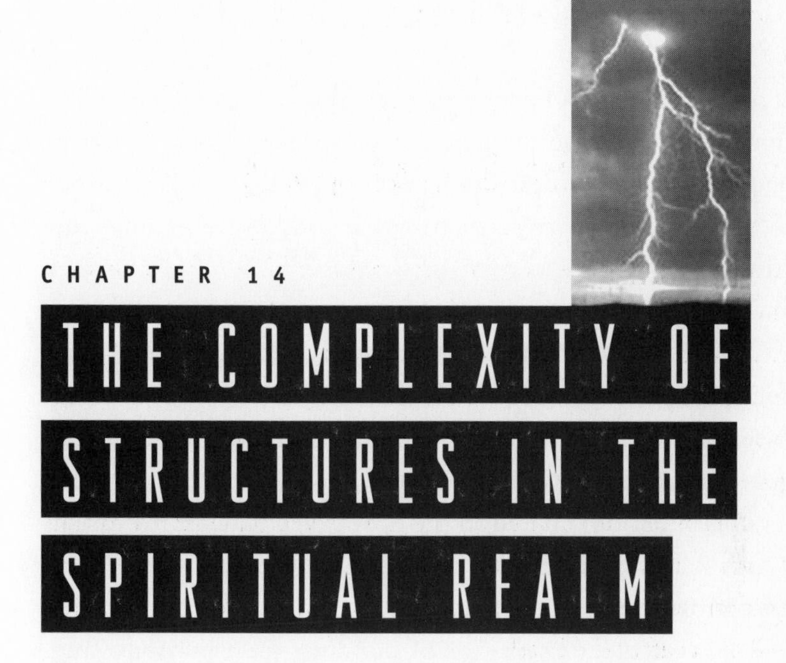

CHAPTER 14

THE COMPLEXITY OF STRUCTURES IN THE SPIRITUAL REALM

In previous chapters we have looked at how Satan constructs demonic strongholds. Now it is important to examine more closely what these structures look like in the enemy's kingdom.

We saw that Satan builds fortified cities through wounding the earth with idolatry, witchcraft and unconfessed sins of bloodshed and social injustice committed by institutions (both religious and secular), governments and ethnic groups. We also saw that sin provides building material for the devil. The fact that there are ancestral covenants that have not been broken allows a structure to be formed in the heavenlies, thus enabling it to release its influence over a city and shackle the people.

Multiplied Layers of Evil

A society that is founded on the remains of a previous civilization continues to accumulate the sin of both. Even if a city or nation is physically destroyed, in the heavenlies it will continue to be a part of a macro-structure that progressively gains more strength.

This is the case of many Latin-American societies that were destroyed by more powerful cultures. For example, the Aztecs and Incas conquered large areas and formed empires that dominated the continent in the past. In turn, these cultures were conquered and destroyed by the Spanish and later by the nationalist republics that put an end to the Spanish control. In the case of North America, native cultures were either wiped out or conquered by the English or the French.

In the Bible, this process of building upon previous kingdoms and covenants is clearly shown in the passage where Daniel describes a dream of King Nebuchadnezzar:

> You looked, O king, and there before you stood a large statue–an enormous, dazzling statue, awesome in appearance. The head of the statue was made of pure gold, its chest and arms of silver, its belly and thighs of bronze, its legs of iron, its feet partly of iron and partly of baked clay. While you were watching, a rock was cut out, but not by human hands. It struck the statue on its

> feet of iron and clay and smashed them. Then the iron, the clay, the bronze, the silver and the gold were broken to pieces at the same time and became like chaff on a threshing floor in the summer. The wind swept them away without leaving a trace. But the rock that struck the statue became a huge mountain and filled the whole earth (Dan. 2:31-35).

Daniel went on to interpret the dream:

> You are that head of gold. After you, another kingdom will rise, inferior to yours. Next a third kingdom, one of bronze, will rule over the whole earth. Finally, there will be a fourth kingdom, strong as iron—for iron breaks and smashes everything—and as iron breaks things to pieces, so it will crush and break all the others. Just as you saw that the feet and toes were partly of baked clay and partly of iron, so this will be a divided kingdom; yet it will have some of the strength of iron in it, even as you saw iron mixed with clay. As the toes were partly iron and partly clay, so this kingdom will be partly strong and partly brittle. And just as you saw the iron mixed with baked clay, so the people will be a mixture and will not remain united, any more than iron mixes with clay (vv. 38-43).

This prophecy, which was fulfilled in the successive rise to power of the Babylonian, Persian, Greek and Roman empires, sheds light on the way in which Satan's empire becomes progressively stronger. Note that Daniel did not see this sequence of kingdoms as four independent figures, although each one was very different from the previous kingdom. The fact that the four kingdoms make up only one statue tells us that far from being destroyed by successive conquests, the statue continued to gain in strength and shape. That is, the destruction of one kingdom by the next did not destroy the statue. The only thing that can do this is the deadly strike of God's kingdom at the statue's base.

For centuries the devil has been adding structure upon structure, just as in Daniel's vision. But now is the time when the Church of God is rising up to destroy the entire empire in the heavenlies.

Diverse Structures and Strategy

Diverse strongholds exist in the kingdom of darkness. Yet the devil has organized them into a single empire from which he moves and controls all the nations. We can think of this dark realm as a kingdom with a central government controlling a wide range of dependent structures. Each nation, depending on its worldly importance and its influence on the rest of the countries, reveals to us the secret of different structures in the spiritual realm.

When we travel to certain parts of the world, we can sense in our spirit how oppression and demonic activity differ and how they are greater in some places than in others. This is very important to recognize when we speak of spiritual warfare, because man's nature is to make formulas that result in cookie-cutter identities that overlook subtle differences. Because one method of spiritual warfare has produced results in one place, some believe it will work in the same way everywhere else. Nothing could be more wrong.

The devil has structures, kingdoms and military compounds that are distinct from one another. If there is one thing the Holy

Spirit in His wisdom wants to show us, it is that we need to pray for spiritual discernment and to develop a perceptive mentality that can distinguish among various methods appropriate for the warfare that faces us. As the forces of light and darkness face each other, success depends upon who has

1. the better strategy,
2. the greater knowledge of the opponent's strengths and weaknesses,
3. the better-organized army and
4. the more powerful weapons.

This order is important. Although as the children of God we know without a shadow of a doubt that we have the more powerful weapons, we have lost many battles, because we did not have the right strategy or know where to attack the enemy. Like a game of chess, we have to anticipate the deceitful moves of our adversary, remaining alert to strategies that check the devil's moves even before he makes them.

Nothing saddens me more than seeing a Christian who has the very armor of the living God, with all the power of the weapons of the all-powerful One at his disposal, fall in defeat because of inadequate knowledge of appropriate strategy or because of inadequate organization. It is discouraging to see Satan, who has already lost the war and is fallen and crushed by the blood of Jesus, hoisting the flag of victory after smaller battles with inadequately armed Christians who have surrendered by default.

Victory in a war requires not only powerful weapons but effective intelligence resources, knowledge and intuition. It is not a matter of launching bombs without thinking and just waiting to see if we hit a stronghold; rather, it is about timing and attacking in key places. For this reason we should not attack all fortified cities in the same way. To make this mistake can be very costly.

A Victory over Multiple Structures

Many times we limit spiritual warfare to the territorial powers of a city or country without taking into account the fact that multiple structures and military compounds exist which inclusively embrace different nations. Not taking this into consideration where it is merited can lead to a counterattack by Satan and failure to take the territory.

Years ago, Dr. Chaves received from God the task of taking the city of Cartago, the most important stronghold in his country of Costa Rica. His strategy culminated with a convention of intercession deep in enemy territory. He began to seek the direction of the Holy Spirit, and God led him to anoint the whole country from north to south and east to west, forming a cross that extended across the whole nation. Accompanied by his battle team, Dr. Chaves climbed one of the highest mountains in the country, a volcano that had been the site of terrible rites of satanism and invocations of the devil. They anointed the city of Cartago, and, standing face-to-face with the image that represented the spiritual patroness of Costa Rica, Dr. Chaves decreed her defeat.

The battle had been carried out completely and precisely. As the date of the convention approached, the battle intensified. Rony, filled with the Spirit of God, was determined to strike a deadly blow. While I was praying for him, the Lord put it in my heart to support this great effort by leading a spiritual warfare team, commandos who would reinforce the last and masterful attack.

I arrived in Costa Rica with my team. Two sisters from Guatemala and four brothers from Cartago joined with us, making a total of 12 warriors. We knew we needed a strategy, and we were willing to fight until we saw this centuries-old power fall. As I was praying to God, the Spirit gave me a Scripture: "Are you better than Thebes, situated on the Nile, with water around her? The river was her defense, the waters her wall. Cush and Egypt were her boundless strength; Put and Libya were among her allies" (Nah. 3:8,9).

Through this word, the Lord showed me that we were dealing with a city fortified by various strongholds and allies and that we would not be able to take Cartago without first eliminating the powers who protected her. The world witnessed an example of this in Saddam Hussein's attack on Kuwait before the Gulf War. In order to obtain victory, Iraq first would have had to attack the United States, which had dedicated itself to protecting the small country of Kuwait. Unable to do this, Saddam suffered the devastation of Desert Storm.

In the case of Cartago, Dr. Chaves managed to get us the city's coat of arms, and through examining its heraldry we were able to discover how to take the city. The shield consisted of a rampant lion, three stripes of blood across it and a castle on its lower part. On the sides of the shield were six eagles with demonic faces. The Lord showed us that these were the six guardians that protected the city. The lion was located inside the Irazu volcano, and the three stripes of blood were the two craters and an enormous esplanade of ash, full of satanic symbols.

Victims had been thrown into one of the craters as sacrifices to Satan. In the second crater we found a cabala–secret magical writing–carved in stones, which we interpreted to mean "the antichrist reigns." The six eagles on the shield were six witchcraft-dominated sites surrounding Cartago, including Rio Reventazon, the riverbed through which the conquistadors entered, bringing with them idol worship. The castle drawn on the shield represented the basilica of the patron of Costa Rica.

Eight years earlier Rony had a vision in which he saw Cartago's main basilica with a huge gorilla inside. He then saw a cloud descend with God's brilliance, and from this cloud a hand came out and grabbed the gorilla and threw it out with great power. Although I knew nothing about this vision at the time, the Lord reminded us of Ezekiel 30:18: "Dark will be the day at Tahpanhes when I break the yoke of Egypt; there her proud strength will come to an end. She will be covered with clouds, and her villages will go into captivity."

On the last day, early in the morning, we set out to take the basilica, represented by the castle on the coat of arms. When dawn began to break, we started to walk around the structure seven times before entering. On the third time around, a supernatural cloud covered the building. It was the only place in the whole city covered by this dark cloud that was so dense that we could not make out a single brick in this great stronghold. Feeling the solemn presence of God's Spirit invading everything, we were overcome with reverence. We knew that the powerful hand of our God was crushing the power of evil. The sixth time around the basilica, the cloud of darkness lifted and disappeared.

Our strategy was largely to depend upon the Holy Spirit and to trust that the victory would come through obedience. We rejoiced in the great triumph and we were grateful for having been allowed a small part in the battle.

From Armadas to Dominions

When I was in Puerto Rico with a group of pastors looking for strategies for how we could take this nation, I was able to discern another kind of stronghold.

We were taking a stroll through the old part of San Juan to try to discern through the history of the place what might be in the heavenlies. When we reached the great fortress, which stood as a powerful bastion on the coast, I could see in the spirit enormous guardians that appeared to be protecting some extremely valuable treasure. There were many of them, like an organized army.

Without knowing what I was seeing in the spiritual realm, one of the pastors commented that Puerto Rico was one of the main ports where the United States Navy is based. It is a key point from which to safeguard the United States from attacks by way of the Atlantic Ocean. This made me think that while in the natural realm Puerto Rico is a maritime defense of the American Navy, in the spiritual realm an organized armada of protectors was also based there. This spoke to me of a stronghold guarding the coasts of the continental United States.

The definitive conclusion came to me after receiving a prophecy that I would soon go to Haiti. At that moment, the Holy Spirit told me: *There are three armories which defend North and Central America. They are Puerto Rico, Haiti and Cuba.* Curiously enough, these three countries are the very nations, along with Brazil in South America, that are the most steeped in magic and the pagan religion of Santeria.

What is interesting here is that the strategies for taking a castle of demonic sentinels such as Dr. Chaves saw over Mexico, the multiple strongholds of Cartago and the armories revealed to me defending North and Central America are all completely different.

The Lord also allowed us to see another spiritual force: a dominion of darkness. Carrying out a battle in Mexico City, which we had code-named Babylon, we were walking through the streets when a brother told us of an indigenous sect called La Mexicanidad to which he had belonged. This man was surprised to find out that the route the Holy Spirit outlined for us to take to undo the ancestral covenants of the city was the exact route the sect used to awaken the gods of the past.

Motivated by this revelation and being a good servant of God, the man drew nearer to tell us about a plan that was being carried out in various American and Asian countries. He told us of a triangle through which thousands of people belonging to this sect (which joins with thousands of other natives and esoteric practitioners in spirit) were sending energy and making incredible invocations to exercise their influence in order to gain the largest number of followers of any of the New Age sects. The points of this triangle are the volcano Popocatepetl in Mexico, Machupichu in Peru and Mount Everest in Nepal and Tibet.

International Connections

Satan may execute his dominion not just over a city or nation but also over one or more countries through networks of evil. According to some, the European Community is the prime example of such a network; and if they are correct, the throne of the Antichrist may even emerge from this union.

In the case of a throne of darkness, let's see how an accurate blow on the enemy's head brings deliverance, even in different places. In a message I listened to given by Cindy Jacobs, she spoke of how a terrible bitterness had existed for centuries between the French and the English in Canada. In a meeting with the goal of reconciliation, participants took part in identificational repentance, in which both French and English asked forgiveness for the sins that had been committed hundreds of years previously by their ancestors. The legal base that had allowed a demonic throne to operate, sending in powers of bitterness, contempt and hatred, was wiped out. Healing could now be brought to the land.

When she returned to her home in the United States, Cindy learned that a large group of French people who had been opposed to the gospel for years had repented and given their lives to Christ. The results of a public event in Canada had overflowed into the personal and spiritual lives of many.

As another example of the international scope of Satan's dominion, the reach of Egyptian magic controls a large number of groups and institutions around the world: New Age practitioners, university students and staff, graphic arts and media professionals, Illuminati, Freemasons and members of sects of African and Caribbean magic.

A throne of occultism has reigned in parts of Europe since the Middle Ages, when sorcery, witchcraft and spiritism flourished. In modern times, Europe has given rise to the Third Reich, the punk rock culture, fan violence at sporting events, international terrorism and social anarchists.

Other associations for evil exist throughout the world, governing those people in highly placed financial sectors who are in charge of making the most important economic decisions both nationally and internationally. In this way, through treaties and Machiavellian maneuvers, Satan is able to raise up worldwide economic moves to oppose righteousness and justice, especially among the poor. These powers include the Club of Rome, the Venetian Mafia, the International Monetary Fund, the Illuminati and the owners and controllers of Swiss banks.

Peter Wagner, speaking on spiritual warfare at the strategic level as it affects the 10/40 Window, said:

> Luis Bush observed that this area was situated between the latitudes of 10° and 40° north and drew a rectangle

> on the map, which he calls "The 10/40 Window." This 10/40 Window is becoming widely accepted by missiologists as the most crucial area for the focus of the forces for world evangelization in the 1990s. Within it are the centers of Buddhism, Confucianism, Hinduism, Islam, Shintoism and Taoism.
>
> George Otis, Jr. says, "By playing host to these religions' nerve centers—and some 95 percent of the world's unreached peoples—the lands and societies of the 10/40 Window can hardly avoid becoming the primary spiritual battleground of the 1990s and beyond. And when the epic conflict finally unfolds, enemy operations will in all likelihood be managed from two powerful strongholds—Iran and Iraq—situated at the epicenter of the Window." Otis points out that strategic-level spiritual warfare seems to be building up at the same geographical location where it started, the Garden of Eden.[1]

I mention these thrones because I know that in the coming years key blows will be struck there that are part of great strategies directed by the Holy Spirit. Just as Dr. Rony Chaves received from God the exact point of attack for delivering his nation, in each country particular places have to be taken. They are like the knots and cords that keep the devil's net of operations strong in a country.

Some places throughout the world are spiritually binding millions of people, impeding the gospel from spreading and enslaving people with spiritual blindness. There are spiritual battles to be fought for our cities. Large evangelistic campaigns and church growth techniques will not prosper as we desire until these knots, or key points, of satanic spiritual government in a country have been taken.

The greater and more influential a country is on the worldly level, the more complex is the net of strongholds and the knots that must be cut. When these points of demonic government are stripped of their power, we will see television stations and public stadiums come into the hands of Christians around the world; and those members of government, leading business people and professionals with the ability to lead thousands out of captivity will come to the feet of Jesus.

Note

1. C. Peter Wagner, *Warfare Prayer* (Ventura, CA: Regal Books, 1997), p. 151.

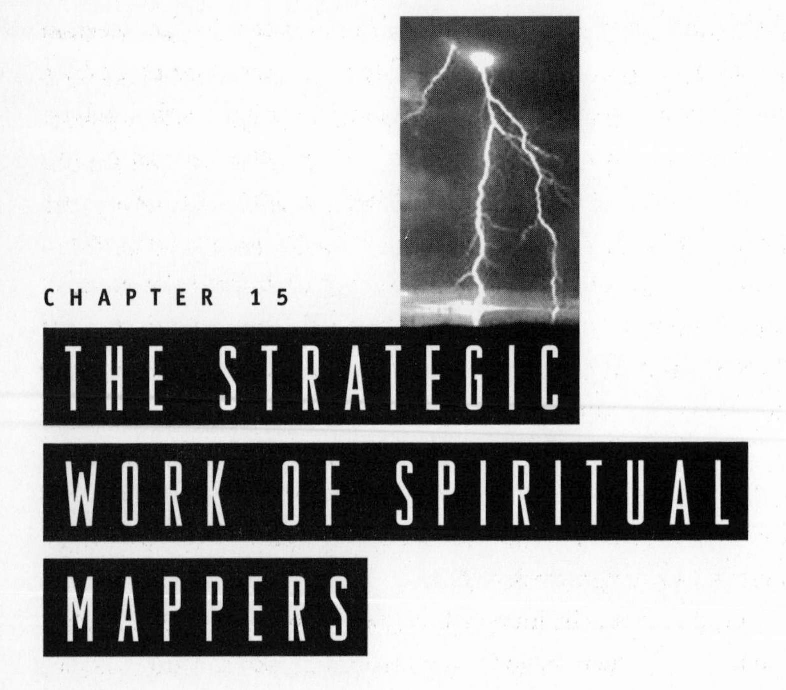

CHAPTER 15

THE STRATEGIC WORK OF SPIRITUAL MAPPERS

It is the work of the Holy Spirit to define war strategies. Let's not forget that He is the supreme general, the One who gives revelation to His servants the prophets. Therefore, prophetic leadership may not be necessary to make prayer walks or to go around a city seven times. Committed prayer groups can usually carry this out without any problem, and they will accomplish effective results.

Indispensable Prophets

There are other areas, thrones and cities, however, that are seats of satanic power where prophetic leadership is definitely indispensable—not only in working out a battle strategy that keeps the soldiers alive but in confronting the powers of darkness in the authority given by God to this ministry. In fact, certain places on a national and worldwide level cannot be taken by a simple prayer group but must be taken by prophets themselves.

Some battles can be delegated, while other key campaigns cannot. For example, only David had the faith, anointing and divine backing to kill Goliath. Only Elijah had the order from God to confront the priests of Jezebel with fire from heaven. Only Solomon was allowed to build the Temple. Only John the Baptist could adequately prepare the way for the Lord. God had other servants during all of these times, and some might want to say that any of God's people could have performed these tasks, but that wasn't the case. Certain orders from God have to be fulfilled by specific people with a specific call at a specific time. This is a sovereign work of God.

God's work is intimately linked with the vessel God has chosen and with the role God has given His chosen servant. It is certain that the move of God today is not limited to a few men and women of God but to the Church as a whole. However, it would be a terrible mistake to think that we all have the same anointing and the same calling, simply because we are all children of God. When I speak of anointing, I am referring to the power of God that comes upon, or over, particular persons to enable them to carry out that for which they have been commissioned. As Paul said: "Are all apostles? Are all prophets? Are all teachers? Do all work miracles?" (1 Cor. 12:29).

The people whom God is choosing for spiritual warfare include generals, captains, intelligence agents and trained soldiers. Maybe you, dear reader, have something to do with this calling. (See the epilogue.)

The Ministry of Mapping

One of the tools of spiritual warfare being revealed by the Holy Spirit is the strategic task of an intelligence corps. These are researchers, or spies, who investigate enemy territory to discover the adversary's weak points and locate his strongholds within neighborhoods, cities, regions, nations and continents. This has come to be called spiritual mapping.

Of course, all strategies should be outlined in prayer and should depend totally on the Holy Spirit. This intelligence corps, however, may also rely on specific tools and strategies of war revealed by the Spirit to His generals. They may delve into the pages of a region's history to discover anything that may be useful in working out a strategy. They outline on maps the most important points where Satan's forces and historical structures are concentrated. What do such leaders look for?

Historical Origins

The Significance of Naming

Satanic captivity may have a significant role in the name of a place. For example, "Tenochtitlan," the original name of what we now call Mexico, means "the navel of the world."[1] This speaks of a throne of central importance and influence, such as the Aztec empire that was and continues to be a center for esoteric and demonic activity.

In his book *Warfare Prayer,* Peter Wagner writes about the names of some spirits. He says:

> We need to recognize that those who deal regularly with the higher levels of the spirit world agree that, while knowing the proper names might not be necessary, it is helpful in many cases. The reason is that there seems to be more power in a name than many of us in our culture might think.[2]

If this is the case, the operating characteristics of a spirit are not made known by invocations of magic or witchcraft. Instead, they may reside within the name!

Spirits in the occult world are invoked by name. The invocations of satanists on rock singers is done by name. Spiritualists call upon the specific names of the dead or of demons to perform healing. Even some who rely on the occult to bet on games of chance invoke spirits by name. The list is unending; and while we as warriors of Christ may not know all these names, one thing is certain: we have *the* Name, which is above every name (see Phil. 2:9) and which is sufficient to make the most ferocious enemy flee.

Yet, with Peter Wagner, I hold the opinion that a powerful force is added to our faith when we know the name of our enemy and rebuke him by name.

A Place's Sphere of Influence

Spiritual mapping strategists may also ask, What sphere of influence does this place, city or region have in the country and in the world?

Here it is fitting to research everything that would be of interest in the light of spiritual battle. What kind of city are we dealing with? Is it a capital? Is it a financially outstanding city? Is it a city known for idolatry and witchcraft? It is also necessary to discover whether there are ruins of ancestral civilizations; places where there have been crimes, killings or inquisitions; sites of earthquakes, cyclones or mass tragedies (since they can be due to ancestral covenants that demand victims or judgments of God for some persistent, serious sin).

It would also be helpful to know what kind of buildings were destroyed in such disasters. For example, a number of tarot card places, brothels and the buildings of corrupt government officials were destroyed in the Mexican earthquake of 1985. These places represent three of the greatest sins of our country. Another case is that of Taras in Costa Rica, which was almost wiped out by a mudslide coming from the volcano Irazu. The blood principality which was established there continues to demand victims and did so in this case by devouring a whole town. In such cases it is essential to ask forgiveness for the city's sin and to cancel ancestral covenants.

The Legacy Symbolically Portrayed on the City's Coat of Arms

In the preceding chapter we noted the importance of this kind of research in spiritual battle. It is urgent to ask how the Holy Spirit interprets these ties to the tradition of heraldry.

This knowledge is determined through established symbols which characterize a name, city or institution and are portrayed on a coat of arms. These symbols are not chosen by accident; they inevitably follow established rules that can be traced to ancient practices, family names and lands.

Heraldry was created as a system of designs for the coat of arms of each house, kingdom, county province, etc. The earliest references suggest that there was a truly direct relationship between the right to bear arms and the ancestral possessions of feudal estates and castles. Only those in battle who owned such a fiefdom commanded a great number of men who carried individually distinct weapons. Remembering the principle that the natural realm has parallels in the spiritual, we may conclude that such symbols bear significance in both worlds.

Values, attributes and symbols represented on a coat of arms identify the dominion and power of each noble house. These were and are the hereditary decrees of a generational line. In some cases, the coat of arms was also a reflection of part of secular history that was represented by a broad range of symbols. Such symbolism was used not only in Europe but also throughout the world on the seals, shields and banners of armies.

In the Bible, the importance of this kind of military symbolism is reflected in one of the names of God: "Jehovah Nissi," which means "The LORD is my banner" (Exod. 17:15). Here we have a picture of God's armies going forth to war under the banner of His Name.

Shields, on which certain national symbols were often engraved, are also mentioned as an important factor in the spirit of military gatherings:

> Men of Arvad and Helech manned your walls on every side; men of Gammad were in your towers. They hung their shields around your walls; they brought your beauty to perfection (Ezek. 27:11).

A popular refrain from the times when Mexico, Tenochtitlan, was founded says:

This is your command,
Oh lord of life!
Remember it, oh princes,
Don't forget it.
Who can besiege Tenochtitlan?
Who can shake the foundations of heaven?
With our arrows,
With our shields,
This city exists.[3]

The spiritual analysis of all these different kinds of symbols—hierarchies of nobility, mythological animals, castles, ferocious beasts, serpents, towers and weapons of war—is one of the interesting parts of heraldry. Many of the animals and mythological creatures (such as mermaids or unicorns) that appear on coats of arms have to do with pagan myths and may be related to territorial spirits.

It is also curious to see the similarities of city shields, even when they are of different countries, raising the question of whether it is by chance or if both cities have similar spiritual traits.

The Moral and/or Religious Tone of an Area's Territorial Heritage

Some spiritual mappers have found it useful to research the background of a territory. Was it a colony with overbearing overlords? Was it a marquisette, a duchy, etc.? What do we know about its early rulers? While researching the city of Monterrey in the state of Nuevo Leon in Mexico, we discovered that the first man to receive that land from the Spanish conquistadors was well known for his greed and sexual promiscuity. Natives of that state have informed us that these are still the two most frequently recurring sins in this city.

Places of Spiritual Influence

Active generals with experience in spiritual mapping for God's intelligence corps have learned the importance of certain geographical features that we would do well to consider as we engage in spiritual warfare.

Mountains or High Places

Mountains are places that are not only spiritual symbols but locations where both the devil and God have often been worshiped. Every time God revealed the blueprints of His design, He chose a man and He chose a mountain.

Mount Ararat, the site where God placed the ark and chose to reveal His plan to Noah, represents a new generation. It was on Mount Sinai where God spoke to Moses, giving him the Law and the whole structure of the Tabernacle in the desert. On Mount Zion, King David built a tabernacle to be filled with the praise and worship to the Most High. Solomon constructed the magnificent Temple of God on Mount Moriah.

The mountain is a symbol of a throne that governs and rules from on high. David said, "To the Lord I cry aloud, and he answers me from his holy hill" (Ps. 3:4). For this reason Satan has designs to take over high places so he can execute his demonic power from on high. The Scripture describing his fall says:

> You said in your heart, "I will ascend to heaven; I will raise my throne above the stars of God; I will sit

> enthroned on the mount of assembly, on the utmost heights of the sacred mountain. I will ascend above the tops of the clouds; I will make myself like the Most High" (Isa. 14:13,14).

Throughout history and even today we see how Satan has established his throne on the high mountains and peaks of cities and nations to govern from on high. Ezekiel describes God's judgment on this practice:

> And they will know that I am the LORD, when their people lie slain among their idols around their altars, on every high hill and on all the mountaintops, under every spreading tree and every leafy oak–places where they offered fragrant incense to all their idols (Ezek. 6:13).

Still, many leaders in Israel persisted in following Satan's leadership to the mountaintops. It is said of King Manasseh:

> He did evil in the eyes of the LORD, following the detestable practices of the nations the LORD had driven out before the Israelites. He rebuilt the high places his father Hezekiah had demolished; he also erected altars to the Baals and made Asherah poles. He bowed down to all the starry hosts and worshiped them (2 Chron. 33:2-3).

During a series of conferences given by Dr. Rony Chaves on the topic of Mexicans in victory, he brought us a seed of revelation regarding mountains that had been planted in our hearts and continued to grow. At that moment God spoke to us, saying that a group of warriors should take the highest mountains in the country.

The first strategy He gave us was to ascend three mountains—Ajusco, Cerro de la Estrella and Tepeyac—which form a triangle of satanic power over the capital. It was a great and novel challenge, since nobody had yet climbed up to intercede on the very place where the devil had built his altars of worship. It also required an unprecedented physical effort.

We organized the climb of Ajusco, the highest of the three mountains—at nearly 12,000 feet. A team led by my sister drove around the great mountain several times. They anointed the entire base of the mountain with oil, poured out wine for the healing of the land, threw salt to seal a new covenant and gave the mountain into the hands of Jesus Christ. I was on the other team, which was assigned the task of climbing to the highest point of the mountain. I thank God, because He is the only One who could have put us on the summit. There was no path to the top, and we had to climb up an almost vertical cliff. While we were climbing, we felt the presence of hundreds of demons, making the hairs on our skin stand on end. Throughout the ascent there were covenants and spiritual guardians that we rebuked and demolished.

When we reached a small plateau just below the highest peak, we discovered a large quantity of human graves where satanists had made sacrifices and buried their victims. It was around the time of Halloween when we made the climb, and some of the graves were still fresh. There were demonic altars on every side which we pulled down and invalidated by the blood of Jesus.

While we were destroying these covenants over the tombs, a black bull appeared on the mountain's summit, staring at us. It was impossible to think that we were dealing with an animal of flesh and blood, since the flattest slopes were at least 45 degrees and in some parts we needed to climb on all fours and use chains to help pull us up. We all knew we were dealing with a power of death that lived in that place. However, we were not afraid, because we were surrounded by an almost tangible presence of the Holy Spirit who said to us, *Do not fear, continue destroying everything.* We did so, and a little while later the bull disappeared.

We divided the team into two groups. One arrived at a deep pass which had a projecting rock pointing toward Mexico from on high. When they reached it, they were not surprised to discover a series of terrible demonic symbols which were all directed toward an arrow pointing at the city. Team members rebuked the symbol with all authority, breaking every covenant. They made every effort to destroy the drawings, and when they left, the place was consecrated to God. The other group reached the summit where there was another altar, which they pulled down.

That time on the summit was one of the moments when I have most felt the power of God flow over me. We were worshiping God, and the Holy Spirit had come down upon us. There was a solemn sense of God's presence and a revelation as to God's name of war which unfolded in the sky in front of us. I then saw a frightening vision: in the heights over the whole length and width of the central valley of Mexico were soldiers of the shining army of God on one side and the troops of the devil's army on the other. At that moment the Lord's voice spoke to me: *Prophesy over my armies, because I have commanded Michael to fight.* My heart almost stopped on seeing that wonder. I felt the power of God as though I were connected to an electrical cable. Without hesitation I released the word and, like a trumpet of war, decreed the attack of God's army on the hosts of the devil. At that moment the sky turned black as in a great storm, and we could hear thunder and see lightning.

A word of the Lord came to me to prophesy at that moment when the two armies were fighting:

> Raise a banner on a bare hilltop, shout to them; beckon to them to enter the gates of the nobles. I have commanded my holy ones; I have summoned my warriors to carry out my wrath—those who rejoice in my triumph. Listen, a noise on the mountains, like that of a great multitude! Listen, an uproar among the kingdoms, like nations massing together! The LORD Almighty is mustering an army for war. They come from faraway lands, from the ends of the heavens—the LORD and the weapons of his wrath—to destroy the whole country (Isa. 13:2-5).

Then a word from Zechariah was added:

> Ask the LORD for rain in the springtime; it is the LORD who makes the storm clouds. He gives showers of rain to men, and plants of the field to everyone. The idols speak deceit, diviners see visions that lie; they tell dreams that are false, they give comfort in vain. Therefore the people wander like sheep oppressed for lack of a shepherd. My anger burns against the shepherds, and I will punish the leaders; for the LORD Almighty will care for his flock, the house of Judah, and make them like a proud horse in battle. From Judah will come the cornerstone, from him the tent peg, from him the battle bow, from him every ruler. Together they will be like mighty men trampling the muddy streets in battle. Because the LORD is with them, they will fight and overthrow the horsemen (Zech. 10:1-5).

The prophetic mantle was over us, and we proclaimed a great revival in Mexico from on high. We released God's Spirit to come from the four cardinal points of the earth. A high place that for years had been an altar of worship to the devil now started to become an altar of worship and throne of praise to the King of kings and Lord of lords, Jesus Christ!

While the lightning flashed over the valley, our song rose to heaven; and in the middle of this glorious presence we raised a golden banner in the highest place which said, "Arise, shine, for your light has come, and the glory of the LORD rises upon you" (Isa. 60:1). We consecrated the place to God, anointed it and sealed it with a salt covenant. We decreed that the place would remain an altar to the God of glory and that whoever would try to profane it with any kind of demonic work would be exposed to rebuke and the judgment of God.

On every mountain we have climbed, we have found abominable things that Satan has used to bring iniquity upon cities. We have been atop mountains where idolatrous statues, crosses, chapels and television antennas have been placed. Such places need to be redeemed by the people of God, since they act as places where demonic government is executed from and from which hundreds of thousands of people are bound.

On the mountain overlooking the city of Rio de Janeiro in Brazil, there is an enormous statue in the form of Christ with His arms open. Millions of people bring offerings to the statue, celebrate it and give it power during the carnivals. However, many locals will tell you that the statue's real name is Oxira-Oxala—the great god of Brazil.

The question often asked is, Why climb the mountains? Can't we just pray from our own homes? My answer is that undoing written decrees, tearing down diabolical altars and discerning what is happening from above can only be done by climbing the mountains. In the same way, there are decrees that can only be released with great power from mountaintops. Isaiah 40:9 says: "You who bring good tidings to Zion, *go up on a high mountain*. You who bring good tidings to Jerusalem, lift up your voice with a shout, lift it up, do not be afraid; say to the towns of Judah, 'Here is your God!'" (emphasis added).

To deliver a bewitched house it is necessary to go there. To break a demonic covenant, sometimes you must go to the place where it was made. When prayer walking to deliver a city, you have to walk the streets of the city. What is the difference, then, in the case of a mountain or any other physical place where Satan has established his throne?

It is true that Jesus sent His word of healing and the centurion's servant was healed (Matt. 8:13). Indeed, there is power in releasing the word, but Jesus did not stop coming forward when there was a need or when demonic oppression called for His presence.

Something incredibly powerful happens when we establish God's kingdom in the devil's own territory.

Rivers, Streams and Fountains

Running waters are symbols of currents of spiritual power. God speaks of the flowing of His Spirit as a river of living water. The celestial city described in the book of Revelation is divided by a river that is none other than the torrent of life from the Spirit (see Rev. 22:1,2). Ezekiel also saw a river of water coming from the altar in the Temple of God, which points to life proceeding from the throne and which is sent out as a great flow of waters (see Ezek. 47:12).

However, not all rivers represent the Holy Spirit. Satan, a good imitator of everything God does, also uses rivers as seats of his influence and power. While planning the warfare strategy for Cartago in Costa Rica, I heard the voice of God say to me, "Dry up the river!" This was repeated several times. At first I had no idea what this meant, so I prayed a lot about it.

On arriving in Costa Rica, I found out how the Spanish had entered the island by the river Reventazon and that the first idolatrous church was built beside this river at a place called Ujarraz, the first capital. From there the capital had moved first to Paraiso and then to Cartago and both of these cities were located on the river. These three places are infested with idolatry and witchcraft that are fed by a constant demonic current. Then I understood the message "Dry up the river!" God was referring to a river of satanic influence.

Praying about this, I came to understand several things. Just as human settlements are established beside rivers and other sources of water because they supply the water that is vital for life, so in the spiritual realm strongholds have supplies of iniquity that sustain them.

For example, a center of idolatry can survive only while it is being fed by sources of witchcraft. The greater the power of Satan that is exercised over an idolatrous place, the greater its fame and the more souls are made captive. Demonic powers are released as torrents of provision for a stronghold, keeping it alive and functioning.

In many battles through the ages, strong cities and fortresses have been taken by the opponent's forces drying up the river which sustained them, eventually forcing surrender for need of water. Because rivers are such an important source of sustenance, some pagan people believe that their watercourses are inhabited by gods and demons. God once gave a word of warning to Egypt, telling the prophet Ezekiel to tell Pharaoh, who was considered a god:

> This is what the Sovereign LORD says: "I am against you, Pharaoh king of Egypt, you great monster lying among your streams. You say, 'The Nile is mine; I made it for

> myself.' But I will put hooks in your jaws and make the fish of your streams stick to your scales. I will pull you out from among your streams, with all the fish sticking to your scales" (Ezek. 29:3,4).

A similar rebuke is given against ravines, through which water often flows, in Ezekiel 6:3,4:

> This is what the Sovereign LORD says to the mountains and hills, to the ravines and valleys: I am about to bring a sword against you, and I will destroy your high places. Your altars will be demolished and your incense altars will be smashed; and I will slay your people in front of your idols.

In his book *Warfare Prayer,* Peter Wagner mentions an experience of the Swedish missionary Kjell Sjoberg in Manaos, Brazil, one of the islands in the middle of the Amazon River:

> As he and other believers prayed that God would reveal to them the strongholds over the area, they visited the famous luxurious Opera House, built by the rubber barons. A huge mural on the stage of the Opera House shows a woman in a river. It turned out to be a representation of the territorial spirit, Iara, the mother of the rivers who ruled the area long before Columbus discovered America. The Opera House had been built as a temple to the goddess Iara.[4]

In the same book, Wagner adds that the Tzotzil people of southern Mexico believe that some of the spirits that inhabit their tribal area and village live in homes and streams.[5]

When I was involved in Santeria (witchcraft), many of the works of magic were offered to Yemaya (considered by some to be the goddess Venus) over the waters of rivers and the sea.

The Rhine River in Germany is a flagrant example of spirits of death in a river. This river has been bathed with blood in countless conflicts and wars. The fact that it is the scene of terrible deaths is undoubtedly why the Rhine occupies a prominent place in German mythology as being occupied by the gods.

The fact that God wants to change such accursed torrents that are the seat of satanic power into fountains of blessing is demonstrated in Ezekiel 32, where God promises through the prophet:

> I will destroy all her cattle from beside abundant waters no longer to be stirred by the foot of man or muddied by the hoofs of cattle. Then I will let her waters settle and make her streams flow like oil, declares the Sovereign LORD. When I make Egypt desolate and strip the land of everything in it, when I strike down all who live there, then they will know that I am the LORD (vv. 13-15).

In Cartago, when I understood what God was telling me about drying up the river, the next question was, Where do you dry up a river? We had been able to physically go to and take every demonic place the Lord had shown us, but this was about drying up something spiritual. I prayed about it until I received a strong conviction that we had to physically go to the ruins of the ancient city of Ujarraz on the river Reventazon, where the first idolatrous temple was built.

If we look at the taking of Jericho from a spiritual point of view as being an example of satanic buildings in the heavens, the river Jordan would be a bastion impeding the stronghold from being taken. The priests had to first dry up the river waters so that the people could pass over on dry land, making it possible to take the great walled city.

In a similar way, the Reventazon River represented the current of witchcraft and iniquity that fed Cartago with evil. It was the scene of death, rape, superstition and magic that had remained impregnated in the heavens– a spiritual, legal pathway for evil. We had to annul all the acts and covenants of that very place which sustained the dragon in the waters in order to change history. If it had been the place where the curse had entered long ago, we now decreed it as the place of the current of life, the river of God, the fountain from which the Word would flow to reach lost souls, the flow of the Spirit and every blessing from on high.

Looking down on the Reventazon from the mountains above it, we saw that it formed the shape of an enormous green snake with its head seated at Ujarraz and its venomous tail in Cartago. But our prayer would bring God's hand to heal the river so that the gospel would be able to reach that formerly impenetrable city.

After worshiping beside the river for a while, I made a walking staff out of a wooden stick and the rest took other sticks so we could enter the river arm-in-arm, forming a human chain. It was just about to rain, and the cold wind that was blowing made it seem as though the water was freezing. I knew something was about to happen, and this motivated me from within.

The current got stronger as we approached the central part of the river. Little by little we ventured deeper into the river and discovered that the bottom was made up of large, round rocks that made the footing treacherous. When it reached the point where the water was almost up to my waist, the current was so strong that it caught hold of me. I barely survived, as the next step was beyond my strength. In a vain attempt to keep my footing, I tried to drive the stick in a little farther forward, but it felt as if it slipped without finding the bottom. It seemed that I would have to turn back, but I could not disobey God's command. I had to go forward in obedience.

With my whole being, I began to pray intensely in the Spirit, knowing that nothing is too difficult for God. At first nothing happened. Then I suddenly felt overcome with conviction and completely safe. I shouted, "In the name of Jesus!" and I thrust myself forward with the stick in front of me. At that moment God fulfilled His promise, and the miracle happened.

Suddenly the momentum of the current, which seemed to be encouraged by hades itself, slowed dramatically. The water actually turned calm, caressing our legs and enabling us to keep our balance without effort and to stand perfectly upright. But this was not enough for our God of grace and love. To our astonishment, the water stopped torturing our muscles with its ice-cold temperature and became warm, almost hot. We were amazed.

We didn't lose any time. We started to rebuke by name all the demons of witchcraft and powers that ruled the city of Cartago. Afterwards, I poured oil on the river and prophesied that the river would be turned into the river of God and that its current would be like the oil of healing. The Lord then told me to take a Bible as a prophetic act and throw it into the river, which I did. As it began to follow the current, the Lord told us to prophesy over it. So we decreed that just as the Bible was being carried along by the river, so the Word of God would be carried through the valley of Cartago.

Finally we decreed that the river of iniquity would dry up forever and in turn would be left open for the armies of God to march forward. I will never forget how the glory of God came down at that moment! God was sending His sign that He was at our side. That miracle was the prelude to all those that would come after and that gave us the final victory over Cartago.

Perhaps the human mind cannot understand this story. It seems crazy, but those of us who experienced it know that the Reventazon was a symbol of what we were entering into and destroying in the kingdom of darkness. Jesus said that we must become like children to enter His kingdom (Matt. 18:3), and from that moment we knew He was holding our hand.

Dr. Rony Chaves, while in Mexico for the Mexicans in Victory conference, was filled with the Holy Spirit and gave a word that was truly fulfilled in our lives at that time. He noted that in Joshua 3:14-17 the priests of Israel had to enter the Jordan River before its flow would stop and allow the rest of the people to cross over. As they entered the waters of opposition, they may have felt that the current was so strong they were going to drown. But what the priests couldn't see was that, 30 kilometers upstream, the river had dried up, allowing the people to cross over triumphantly on dry ground. Rony said that God is still seeking men and women who would dare to get their feet wet!

While this message was obviously directed in a spiritual sense to those brave ones who dare to conquer rivers in changing the destinies of nations, we found ourselves physically living it out 30 kilometers from Cartago. Time will pass, and perhaps nobody will know what happened in Reventazon when we set fire to the waters, burning up the evil rooted in the past, so the people could walk on dry ground today. But the testimonies of revival will speak of what was achieved in intimate secret communion between God and a group of people who knew how to believe in Him.

The Seas

Throughout the history of mankind, seas have been considered magical places. They have inspired mythologies, legends and places of worship. The historian Fernando Benitez wrote:

> Huicholes, Tepeehuanes and Nahuas still sing the myth of the frog and they all keep the myth of the serpent which lives in the nocturnal water and threatens to flood the world. The boy star of the morning and the cultural hero kills it with his arrows but as the serpent is immortal, he stands guard with the goal of wiping it out every time it tries to leave the sea and the swamplands.[6]

We see this same dragon, or serpent, in the Bible. Ezekiel 32:2 refers to it in a prophecy against Egypt:

> Son of man, take up a lament concerning Pharaoh king of Egypt and say to him: "You are like a lion among the nations; you are like a monster in the seas."

And Isaiah says,

> In that day, the LORD will punish with his sword, his fierce, great and powerful sword, Leviathan the gliding serpent, Leviathan the coiling serpent; he will slay the monster of the sea (Isa. 27:1).

Other mysterious passages in the Bible speak of monsters with several heads and of Leviathan, which nobody has been bold enough to awaken (see Job 3:8, 41:1). A verse that captures my attention when I meditate on the different strongholds in the world is Isaiah 23:4:

> Be ashamed, O Sidon, and you, O fortress of the sea, for the sea has spoken: "I have neither been in labor nor

given birth; I have neither reared sons nor brought up daughters."

The context of the passage seems to indicate the coming judgment upon the cities along the seacoast, but it also suggests the unknown possibility of a territorial stronghold within the sea itself.

Many sea gods such as the well-known Neptune of the Romans have been widely worshiped. Mexico has a famous statue under the water of the sea of Acapulco and another under the water at the beach of Chancanab in Cozumel. It is not surprising that superstitious fishermen sink images into the sea, so their catch will be blessed.

While I was in Peru studying the ancestral gods of the Incas before giving a conference on spiritual warfare in Lima, I discovered a revealing story of the Peruvian seas. The god Pachacamac, son of the sun, cut up the first woman (of Inca origin), the mother of Vichama. Fleeing the scene of the crime, he jumped into the sea, where his temple is located. Today this place is known as Pachacamac, and three rocks jutting out in front of the coast are worshiped for the three ancient gods Pachacamac, Cauillaca and Vichama.

Swamps and Lagoons

Only three verses in the Bible refer to swampland, and all three seem to indicate that swamps are accursed places. Promising judgment against Babylon, God cursed the land, saying, "I will turn her into a place for owls and into swampland; I will sweep her with the broom of destruction" (Isa. 14:23). In the vision of the great river of God in Ezekiel 47:11, the prophet declares, "But the swamps and marshes will not become fresh; they will be left for salt."

One of the leading places where witchcraft is carried out in Mexico is at the famous Lagoon of Catemaco in Veracruz, where it is reported that sorcerers walk on water and the devil materializes every year during Holy Week and on the Day of the Dead. This is without a doubt one of the most important places that needs to be delivered if we are to see a marvelous revival in Mexico.

Forests

The Bible says in 1 Kings 14:23 that the people "set up for themselves high places, sacred stones and Asherah poles on every high hill and under every spreading tree." Many pagan people have long considered forests to be magical places. The woods of many lands are the epicenters of numerous legends. They are hiding places for witches and places of witchcraft par excellence.

As children, most of us heard tales of enchanted forests where goblins and fairies met and where medieval magicians lived and witches cast their spells. That which appears to be only fantasy is also true. Forests are places that have been chosen for their mysterious shadows and the beautiful play of light filtering through the trees to inspire those who have reached the farthest depths of magic. Frequently witches as well as sorcerers bury their work in forests, and witches' sabbaths are held in these places. They are also a favorite place for satanists to carry out their killings and mutilations.

My sister and I went to preach at a place near Salem, Massachusetts, and only on a very few occasions have we felt such demonic oppression as we did there. Due to this oppression, the people of this area were extremely aggressive toward the Word of the gospel—to the point of calling the police because we were evangelizing in a park. Some people became so infuriated they almost struck us, because we told them that Jesus loves them. This obviously speaks of a sphere of captivity where demonic forces had totally blinded the inhabitants.

One of the peculiarities of Salem's history is that people who were involved in witchcraft showed great hatred toward Christians, because wherever the servants of the Most High met to pray, the land and its plants lost all of their magical powers.

The house where we were staying was located in the middle of a forest. From the moment we arrived, we began to discern terrible satanic activity coming from the undergrowth. It wasn't until we decided to go out and do spiritual warfare, breaking every covenant of witchcraft in that forest, that we were able to sleep. The battle we undertook was a key to what God would later show us.

Forests are strategic places, being natural refuges for the construction of strongholds. Speaking of Jotham, king of Judah, the Word says that "he built towns in the Judean hills and forts and towers in the wooded areas" (2 Chron. 27:4). Although Jotham was a king who "did what was right in the eyes of the LORD" (v. 2), I want to make note of his construction of forts and towers in wooded areas—places likely to attract those who would set up strongholds of Satan as well.

When Jesus gave John the vision of the seven churches in the book of Revelation, he said to the church at the city of Pergamum, "I know where you live—where Satan has his throne" (Rev. 2:13). Tradition has it that a forest lay just outside the city and that an enormous sanctuary to Æsculapius, god of healing, which surely was a center of important demonic activity, was located there.

The forest of Chapultepec in Mexico City is one of the places most visited by occult sects. In fact, there is a site there where satanists recruit and then kill children taken from the streets.

This has been one of the places where the battle we have had to fight has been the hardest.

I want to make it clear that not all seas, swamps, rivers, mountains and forests are occupied by territorial spirits. In their pristine state, they are a part of the creation that God pronounced as being very good. We should treat such natural resources as treasures, guarding and protecting them from being ravaged both spiritually and physically. Yet we should also be aware that their very attraction sometimes draws the forces of Satan to locate strongholds there.

Notes

1. "Who Were the Aztecas and Who Were the Mexicas?" http://www.azteca.net/aztec/mexica.html (accessed July 2000).
2. C. Peter Wagner, *Warfare Prayer* (Ventura, Calif.: Regal Books, 1997), p. 148.
3. Source unknown.
4. Wagner, *Warfare Prayer,* 145.
5. Ibid., p. 147.
6. *Historia de la Ciudad de Mexico* (Mexico City: Salvat Mexicana de Ediciones S.A. de C.V., 1984), p. 41.

CHAPTER 16

WEAPONS IN THE PALACE OF THE FOREST

The prophet Isaiah once portrayed God as lamenting that His people were found weaponless during an attack by their enemies: “The defenses of Judah are stripped away. And you looked in that day to the weapons in the Palace of the Forest” (Isa. 22:8). This Palace of the Forest was apparently an armory built by King Solomon out of the mighty cedars from the forest of Lebanon (see 1 Kings 7:1-3). The point here is that God’s people were rendered helpless, because the palace, or armory, had been raided by the enemy, and the weapons that had been stored there were no longer available.

Obviously it is essential that those who engage in spiritual warfare know what weapons are available to them from God's armory and how to use them. It is useless to have high-caliber, sophisticated weapons if the soldiers do not know how to use them.

God has provided us with a suit of glorious armor which is nothing more and nothing less than His own armor: "Finally, be strong in the Lord and in his mighty power. Put on the full armor of God so that you can take your stand against the devil's schemes" (Eph. 6:10,11).

Taking the Offensive

Weapons can be divided into two categories: defensive and offensive. The Church has traditionally maintained a firm defensive position against the devil. I am convinced, however, that the time has arrived when God wants us to understand that there is no better defense than to attack!

God is laying bare the foundations of worldly structures so that the Church can attack the gates of hell in a direct offensive against the satanic government. When we speak of God's armor as described in Ephesians, we should have in mind not a piece of clothing that we casually put on and take off but the actual spiritual weapons God has provided. *The Amplified Bible* implies a much more warlike use of God's armor than we often conceive:

> Therefore put on God's complete armor, that you may be able to resist *and* stand your ground on the evil day [of

danger], and, having done all [the crisis demands], to stand [firmly in your place]. Stand therefore [hold your ground], having tightened the belt of truth around your loins and having put on the breastplate of integrity *and* of moral rectitude *and* right standing with God. And having shod your feet in preparation [to face the enemy with the firm-footed stability, the promptness, and the readiness produced by the good news] of the Gospel of peace. Lift up over all the [covering] shield of saving faith upon which you can quench all the flaming missiles of the wicked [one]. And take the helmet of salvation and the sword that the Spirit wields, which is the Word of God" (Eph. 6:13-17, emphasis added).

In the original, the Greek for "stand your ground" is from the word *antistenai*, which does not mean to passively resist but rather to oppose, to stand up and confront.

We do not put on and take off God's armor any more than we put on and take off Christ. Once we have clothed ourselves with Christ (see Gal. 3:27), we live and move and have our being in Him. God's armor is the everyday clothing of the soldiers in His army. By the simple act of being the children of God, we possess all His virtue, all His power and all that He is. However, this is not seen until our spiritual life develops and His anointing becomes noticeable in our life as His soldier.

We are like children. In a child's genetic makeup are all the information and all the potential of what he will become when he grows up, even though these traits are not seen until he reaches maturity. In the same way, our armor develops in resistance, power and skill as we wield our spiritual weapons and grow strong in the power of His might: "In conclusion, be strong in the Lord [be empowered through your union with Him]; draw your strength from Him [that strength which His boundless might provides]" (Eph. 6:10, *AMP*).

To the measure we grow in fellowship with Him, allowing Him and His life to be manifested through us, so our armor is seen to be stronger and more radiant in each battle.

A Chink in My Armor

Some time ago, I had a somewhat unpleasant but incredibly revealing experience. My faith is well established upon 1 John 5:18: "We know that anyone born of God does not continue to sin; the one who was born of God keeps him safe, and the evil one cannot harm him." This passage has been the source of incredible courage coming from God and that courage has allowed me to challenge true powers of darkness without any fear of reprisal.

One morning I was preparing for a wedding. Everybody in the church loved the bride and groom as dearly as if they were family. Without realizing it, I had let my guard down by becoming caught up in all the worries of the ceremony. The devil tripped me up, and I got angry with one brother who had made a mess while looking for some things.

Those who know me know that I am usually a calm person and that it is difficult for someone to make me mad. I dearly adore my relationship with the Holy Spirit. But I admit that on this occasion I sinned by becoming angry. I felt the pain immediately, knowing that I had both offended my brother in Christ and grieved my greatest love, my beloved God. I asked for forgiveness straightaway, and on the surface it was as if nothing had happened. But I was to discover later that Satan had taken advantage of this chink in my spiritual armor.

That evening I flew to Monterrey for a conference on divine healing. When I had finished praying for the sick, a prayer warrior with a strong ministry of intercession came up to me and said, "Let me pray for you, because I have seen a woman firing darts at you throughout the whole sermon." I accepted prayer, even though I was sure the devil wouldn't touch me.

However, after leaving there, I began to feel sick. My throat felt as though it was on fire, and my whole body felt like it had been brought down with a fever. The next day, after the conference, I had to go to bed as I could no longer stand the malaise. While trying to rest, I had a dream in which I saw myself fighting with one lion after another. I woke up exhausted from so much fighting and I said to the Lord, "What is this? Why are there so many lions, Lord?"

The Holy Spirit told me, *Because the power in the city is a lion and it is seated on a mountain and its name is the New Lion and it devours queens and maidens.* Hearing this, I realized this was not just a regular dream but something from God. The Spirit then added, *Daughter, where do the lions attack?*

"The throat, Lord," I answered. It was then so clear that God was telling me that I had been attacked by this power. My question was "But why did it touch me, Lord, if Your Word says that the evil one cannot harm me?"

The Lord then opened my spiritual eyes and showed me my armor. I saw a very thick shell of divine life surrounding me. It was about a meter thick, glorious, and it shone like fire. But a hole could be seen in the armor, a rift like the hole which air pollution has created in the ozone layer above the earth.

The Lord said to me, *Look what you did! You made that hole two days ago when you got mad at that brother. The armor I gave you is impenetrable and invincible, but you made a hole in it.* I began to weep. In the visible world, everything had been fixed in just a few minutes; but the damage done in the spiritual realm would take time to repair.

"How can it be repaired?" I asked the Lord.

He answered, *It is mended by letting my life flow. Each time it flows through you, the hole will gradually be filled up until it is restored. But this won't be straightaway; your armor was very strong.*

What a hard and clear lesson! I will never forget the vision of the perforated armor or the lash of that lion's claws, which took so long to heal.

A Symbolic Sword

Intercessory prayer, fasting and declaring the written Word are all well-known weapons that make up part of the Christian's war chest. However, in these last days that are characterized by spiritual battle, the Lord is revealing many other weapons as well. While we were taking Cartago, in Costa Rica, God revealed an unusual example of these weapons in the form of a sword symbolizing His mighty power.

As I have mentioned previously in a discussion of military strongholds and thrones, God had revealed through prophecy that the principality over Cartago was named the prince of Egypt. Coming down the slope of the Irazu volcano after an impressive battle which took place in the crater, we reached a suitable place for continuing the fight. We were still high enough to see the majestic form of the entire Cartago valley. At our feet, the volcano seemed to have been dressed with a thick blanket of yellow flowers. The place couldn't have been prettier.

When we left the capital, the dance team from the Centro Cristiano de San Jose (Christian Center of San Jose, Dr. Rony

Chaves's congregation) had lent us a couple of plastic swords, which they used in drama performances. We took them to use as faith expanders. Logically speaking, a plastic sword can't do anything against the devil. But for a warrior full of the Holy Spirit, holding a symbolic sword in his hands helps him feel the real sword in his hands: the invisible and invincible Word of God (see Eph. 6:17), enabling him to fight in a much more powerful way. (Again, I emphasize that such articles have no power in themselves but only symbolize God's power.)

When we anointed the army, God had prophesied that a sister called Lidia would receive a flaming sword in her hands and that another soldier, Olguita, of fragile appearance but with a heart of steel, would have a scythe in her hands. So I gave these two warriors the two plastic swords as a sign of the power of the spiritual weapons that God had truly given to us, although they couldn't be seen by the natural eye.

When I got out of the Jeep at the volcano, I realized I had forgotten that one such sword was at my side. I took it, knowing it would be useful while decreeing the prophetic word. We needed to prophesy all of Ezekiel chapters 29 through 32 from the top of the volcano. But it was Ezekiel 32:11,12 which changed my whole vision in regard to weapons: "For this is what the Sovereign LORD says: '*The sword of the king of Babylon will come against you*. . . . They will shatter the pride of Egypt'" (emphasis added).

Filled with the Spirit, we proclaimed this word at the top of our voices. As we did so, I lifted up the sword in my hand, and a powerful anointing fell on me. I felt that what I had in my hands was not a plastic toy but a supernatural weapon that God had placed into my hands, a prophetic implement of war forged especially for destroying this prince of Egypt. While prophesying, I waved the sword with full conviction that this weapon was causing deep damage and that its nonexistent edge was sharper than a razor and was causing destruction in the spiritual world.

It was a new sensation. Never before in battle had I felt that I was holding in my hands a powerful weapon that God was giving me. The most marvelous thing of all was that while fighting I glanced around at the rest of the troops and was surprised to see that *both Olguita and Lidia were holding their own swords.* God had placed in my hands a *third* sword with the same innocent appearance of the other two!

How true the oft-spoken phrase "looks are deceiving" really is. People would probably have laughed to see us brandishing plastic swords. But I know for certain that Satan wasn't laughing. He was trembling with fear, because he could see the real sword of the Spirit hidden behind the plastic one. He could see that I held a true symbol of a very real supernatural sword—the sword of the king of Babylon (see v. 11).

This event impacted the entire congregation of Christian Center in San Jose, since they knew they had only given us two swords. God was beginning to weave for us a marvelous revelation regarding prophetic weapons in the last days. This revelation continued to grow until it broke forth as an incredible truth on arriving at the convention of intercession in Cartago. At one of the sessions, when it was my turn to preach, such a powerful anointing descended that I could not begin to bring the message I had prepared. I could only prophesy, giddily releasing everything the Holy Spirit was bringing to my lips. Suddenly He spoke:

Behold, I am removing the covering from Judah, and I am revealing the weapons of the palace in the forest.

At that moment God revealed to me the palace not just built by wood from the forests of Lebanon but an armory in the heavens. It was filled with the most unlikely weapons, but each one had a specific use for pulling down strongholds and destroying the worst enemies. I was seeing something glorious; and it was for this reason that He had given me the plastic sword that proved to be a prophetic weapon, the sword of the king of Babylon, a weapon from God's own arsenal.

This was symbolic of the sword of God that had one day been placed over Nebuchadnezzar to destroy Egypt. Now God was giving it to the Church. And at the moment I saw this, the auditorium was filled with angels who started to distribute weapons to all those who wanted them. There were powerful hammers, chariots of fire, shields reddened with burning fire, brooms with bristles that rip apart, blazing spears, whips, hooks, armor of shining gold, bronze bows, dazzling arrows and axes. God was equipping His people with a new power in battle. Glory to God!

Don't Laugh

If you have read this book up to this point, I doubt very much if you consider what I have just related as a joke. But perhaps what happened was so incredible, so fantastic, so marvelous that you are thinking that my imagination was playing a trick on me. You have every reason and every right to choose whether to believe me or not, whether to laugh or take all this seriously. If I were you, I wouldn't laugh. Just as James says regarding the demons who believe in God and tremble (see Jas. 2:19), I affirm that the hosts of evil know what these weapons are. They are real, and more than one demon has felt them before disappearing into the abyss.

Other Weapons of Our Warfare

The Bible mentions several weapons that are now made available to God's army. We can use them to trample on snakes and scorpions and over all the power of the enemy, and nothing will harm us (see 1 John 5:18). Perhaps they won't appear physically in your hands like that sword did in my hands there on the mountain, but they will be just as real and effective. We walk by faith, and we receive God's weapons by faith.

Without presenting an extensive study at this point, here are some of the weapons that we can prophetically decree to destroy the enemy.

Prophetic Weapons

Some of the weapons mentioned in prophetic passages that warn the wicked of God's militant judgment could be adapted to symbolic use, as the swords we used on the volcano overlooking Cartago.

The War Club

Through the prophet Jeremiah, God said that the people of Israel "are my war club, my weapon for battle—with you I shatter nations, with you I destroy kingdoms" (Jer. 51:20).

Reddened Shields and Flashing Chariots

Speaking of the soldiers of God, the prophet Nahum sees that "the shields of his soldiers are red; the warriors are clad in scarlet. The metal on the chariots flashes on the day they are made ready" (Nah. 2:3). The reference here may be to the soldiers' having colored their shields red as a sign that they are prepared to shed enemy blood.

Horns and Hoofs

God says, "Rise and thresh, O Daughter of Zion, for I will give you horns of iron; I will give you hoofs of bronze and you will break to pieces many nations" (Mic. 4:13). In a spiritual sense, God promises to equip His people, imagined here as a wild bull with metal hooves and horns that will withstand all opposition.

Whips, Clattering Wheels, Galloping Horses, Jolting Chariots and Spears

Again the prophet Nahum foresees the battle against principalities and powers in heavenly places, as recorded in Nahum 3:2,3: "The crack of whips, the clatter of wheels, galloping horses and jolting chariots! Charging cavalry, flashing swords and glittering spears! Many casualties, piles of dead, bodies without number, people stumbling over the corpses."

The Sword

God gives His people spiritual "swords," or weapons, described in language that should put to rest any lingering doubts about the need for prayer warriors to be aggressive and on the attack, not just passive observers of the cosmic battle going on around them:

> You therefore, son of man, prophesy, and clap your hands together; and let the sword be doubled the third time, the sword for the slain. It is the sword for the great one slain, which surrounds them, that their hearts may melt, and many fall at all their gates. I have given the glittering sword. Ah! It is made for striking like lightning, it is wrapped up in readiness for slaughter. Show yourself sharp, go to the right; set yourself; go to the left, wherever your edge is appointed. I shall also clap My hands together, and I shall appease My wrath; I, the LORD, have spoken (Ezek. 21:14-17, *NASB*).

Hooks and Bits

God's word against Sennacherib, king of Syria, is recorded in Isaiah 37:29: "Because you rage against me and because your insolence has reached my ears, I will put my hook in your nose and my bit in your mouth, and I will make you return by the way you came." This speaks of the way a hook in the nose of an ox and a bit in the mouth of a horse forces the animal to the bidding of a workman or warrior. Again keeping in mind a spiritual application, not a fleshly one in which we coerce anyone, this imagery is another way of portraying the victory God's armies are promised over His enemies.

Brooms of Destruction

In Isaiah 14:23 God issues a solemn warning against the Babylonian oppressors of Israel: "I will turn her into a place for owls and into swampland; I will sweep her with the broom of destruction." Here is a symbol that is readily available in the households of God's prayer warriors, who could effectively use them to portray the judgment of God against evil.

Threshing Sledge with Teeth

As the tiny Jewish nation trembled before its enemies, God encouraged His people by saying, "See, I will make you into a threshing sledge, new and sharp, with many teeth. You will thresh the mountains and crush them, and reduce the hills to chaff" (Isa. 41:15). Imagine the effect if in a spiritual battle, a farmer who is one of God's soldiers were to pull behind his tractor a mower whose teeth symbolize the way God will mow the rank weeds sown by the evil one!

Bow and Flaming Arrows

The psalmist warns that "if [God] does not relent, he will sharpen his sword; he will bend and string his bow. He has prepared his deadly weapons; he makes ready his flaming arrows" (Ps. 7:12,13).

Battering Rams and Axes

In Ezekiel 26:9 God's enemies are warned of the weapons to be used against them: "He will direct the blows of his battering rams against your walls and demolish your towers with his weapons."

Weapons of Intercession

Certain types of prayer, praise and other corporate expressions can be used as offensive weapons against the enemy. Some groups have developed praise and war dance ministries which they can explain far better than I, so here I will limit this discussion to other symbolic acts that can be effective in intercessory demonstrations.

Trampling Underfoot

Jesus said, "I have given you authority to trample on snakes and scorpions and to overcome all the power of the enemy; nothing will harm you" (Luke 10:19). To trample means to knock or bring down, to humiliate and stamp under our feet. The act of trampling seems very similar to marching, but it is more aggressive. You *step* on a rug but you *trample* a scorpion. While marching marks the boundaries of a territory, trampling crushes and destroys the power of the enemy under our feet. When we enter a terribly satanic place to take it for Christ, we do so trampling it underfoot, believing that our feet in Christ are His very feet of burnished bronze (see Rev. 1:15) which are destroying the devil.

Shouting

Speaking of the judgment against Babylon, Jeremiah 51:14 says, "The LORD Almighty has sworn by himself: I will surely fill you with men, as with a swarm of locusts, and they will shout in triumph over you."

Shouting is extremely powerful in the spiritual world, because it contains within it an authority and a fear that bind spirits. We realize this when someone shouts at us with authority—we immediately feel bad, our soul is affected, and there is a power that is difficult to resist. When the shout is at the level of the soul, it is much more radical—especially since the enemy is not going to hear the voice of men when Christian warriors shout but the very voice of Christ which is wrapped up in the echoing of our voices.

One of the most powerful battles God has allowed me to organize was on a national level. All over the Republic of Mexico, war groups from each state and hundreds of villages took part in the surrounding of our cities for seven days. This was done simultaneously throughout the whole country, and on the last day we went around the cities seven times.

To finish, all of the teams throughout the land shouted a *shabach* (Hebrew "praise," as in Dan. 2:23) of victory in the central square of their city at the same time. This shout was so powerful in the heavenly realms that at that very time the volcano Popocatepetl became active, and from that day the corrupt leaders in our country began to fall. We experienced a victory like that of Israel when they gave a shabach when they took the city of Jericho (see Josh. 6).

Clapping hands

This weapon of war is mentioned in Ezekiel 6:11:

> This is what the Sovereign LORD says: Strike your hands together and stamp your feet and cry out "Alas!" because

> of all the wicked and detestable practices of the house of Israel, for they will fall by the sword, famine and plague.

Cindy Jacobs says clapping hands is a powerful weapon for breaking yokes.[1]

Laughing

Cindy Jacobs also describes the effect of laughter as an intercessory weapon. She notes that laughter provides (1) personal protection and emotional health and (2) a means of direct warfare against Satan. She explains:

> What does laughter have to do with intercessory praise? It breaks the power of the enemy to depress and oppress you in the midst of battle. Depression dilutes your spiritual strength. Non-biblical studies have shown how laughter works like medicine. Deep laugher oxygenates the blood and causes positive physical changes. . . . Laughter in warfare mocks the enemy. Psalm 37:12,13 says: "The wicked plots against the just, and gnashes at him with his teeth. The Lord laughs at him, for He sees that his day is coming."[2]

Without doubt, laughter is one of the most important provisions for our spiritual strength. It is not in vain that the Word says: "The joy of the LORD is your strength" (Neh. 8:10).

While fighting in Cartago, we were incredibly strengthened by the anointing of laughter which accompanied us every day for as long as the battle lasted. Every evening when it was time to drive back, God gave us a reason to burst out laughing. There were nights when we almost needed to ask for mercy as our stomachs hurt from laughing so hard. This laughter came from God and not only filled us with spiritual strength but with physical strength as well.

The same thing happened when we climbed the Popocatepetl volcano. We had to go up at 3 A.M., and we hadn't been able to sleep even for a minute due to the battle. The Lord released a powerful anointing of laughter upon us, and it enabled us to climb the 17,000 feet up the mountain, none of us having the natural ability to do so.

Everyone involved in the ministry of warfare needs to learn to laugh. Those who are devoted to deliverance need to laugh the most, because the devil is terribly humiliated and put down when the children of God laugh in his face.

Notes

1. Cindy Jacobs, *Possessing the Gates of the Enemy,* Spanish ed. (Miami, FL: Editorial Betania, 1991), p. 145.
2. Ibid., pp. 185, 186.

CHAPTER 17

DISARMING THE POWERS

Doing spiritual battle is nothing less than partnering with God in the triumph He has already gained through Christ. The apostle Paul wrote that Jesus "disarmed the powers and authorities" and "made a public spectacle of them, triumphing over them by the cross" (Col. 2:15). Yet we do not yet see everything put under the feet of the victor (see Heb. 2:8). The war has been won, but the mopping up operation continues; and it is in this occupation army that God honors His servants with commissions.

In this chapter, I would like to share how we were personally launched into this great battle, how everything began. Perhaps God is calling you to take your country, your city or your neighborhood; and these words will be a breath of inspiration for you to take the first step.

A Call to Take a City

It all began one night when Dr. Rony Chaves gave an incredibly prophetic message regarding spiritual warfare and Mexico City. It was one challenge after another that we would dare to take the city. He spoke with power, and through the Spirit, outlined a glorious strategy for taking the Mexican capital.

Piercing my heart like a spear of fire, Dr. Chaves said that if there were only one person present whom the Spirit could rouse to take the first step, God would take the nation for Christ. Armies of thousands of people were not needed, he said. What was needed were 30 brave people like the needy at Adullam's cave who were the foundation of the most powerful army Israel ever had. These warriors, together with their leader, King David, subdued all their enemies and delivered a kingdom of peace to Solomon (see 1 Chron. 11:10-47). "God needs only 30 brave ones who will dare to take up the challenge," Dr. Chaves said.

At that point our church was very young, having only some 50 members. Yet that was many more than the number that Rony said God needed to take the city. The challenge became something feasible, something we could take hold of.

My sister, Mercedes, also has a beautiful congregation and serves God through Ministerios de Amor (Ministries of Love), a ministry dedicated to saving children from the streets. She and several members of her ministry were at the meeting and were also strongly impacted by these words. A few days later she phoned me and said, "I have decided to take up the challenge, and I am going to organize a convoy of cars to surround the city."

It seemed marvelous to me, so I told her that I would organize prayer meetings throughout the city and warfare commandos to take the most strategic sites.

God revealed to the deliverance team that certain pillars of iniquity were holding up a large stronghold of Satan, that there were centers of sin where powers of satanic government were seated that were the structure and foundation of the power of the prince of darkness over Mexico.

We began to study Mexican history. We found the oldest plans of the city and started to compare them with a current map. The Lord showed us that the 24 pillars were the main foundations of iniquity and that they were supporting false walls, just as in a house. God said that 24 is the number of government and that in tearing down these pillars we would have the victory.

In Ranks Around the City

We had to take some terrible places like the market of Sonora. This is the market of witchcraft that supplies objects for magic to a large part of the country. There were other inaccessible places such as the president's mansion, called Los Pinos. Some places we had to take during the night, when we would make seven final laps around the city. Others we were able to take during the day.

Through the ministry of Gwen Shaw, a famous general of prayer, Mercedes learned how to fight using flags inscribed with Bible verses on war and on the glory of God. We made a large number of flags in different colors that would be taken in cars making up a convoy. We took hundreds of small rocks with passages from the Word of God written on them to serve as markers on the ground we were taking.

Everything was ready and the time was set: four o'clock in the morning on seven consecutive days. Faithful brothers came from as far as 80 kilometers from Mexico City to make up part of the caravan.

Each night the battle grew more intense. It was as though an invisible wall of power was being raised up around the city each time, strengthening and establishing the kingdom of heaven. The caravan was like a flaming arrow piercing the city. We drove around with our signal lights on and enormous banners waving from the car windows. It was spectacular to see.

We drove in ranks somewhat like those organized by Joshua when Jericho was taken. First came the cars of praise. Behind them were those of intercession, crying out for the sin of the nation and covering the army from the devil's darts. Then came the pastors, who were worshiping, symbolizing the presence of God in the Ark of the Covenant. They were the ones who poured oil all around the city. Finally came the rest of the spiritual warfare team, shouting against all the demons.

There were visions of angels riding along with their swords drawn above the cars. On the last night everyone in the cars, without exception, heard the shout of the demons who had been locked up and were in great torment.

One morning, one of the elders of a church had been awakened at two o'clock to intercede for the convoy. While praying, he heard the desperate shouts of a possessed woman on the streets. He put his head out of the window to see where the shouts were coming from; and he heard the demon who had possessed this woman shouting aloud: "Help, help, help me, because the cars are getting ready to come out and they are really hurting me!"

Targeting Witchcraft

The next-to-last day arrived, and we went to key places that were to be taken during the day. Perhaps the most impacted was the witchcraft market. We entered the place at six o'clock in the morning. I was leading the operation since I was familiar with the place, having been involved in Santeria before the Lord delivered me. I had a vague memory of the location of the ruling power of darkness at this center of evil, and we began the search.

Seven pastors went into the marketplace, while a group of intercessors furtively surrounded the market. After going up and down the aisles for a while, I gave up and decided to ask where the Patrono de los Miserables (Patron of the Wretched) was. The witches were wary and didn't answer, no doubt feeling that they were dealing with either an intruder or a novice. So I asked them in the language of the santeros. One of the sorcerers understood my question and pointed out the place to us.

We turned halfway around to follow his directions, when suddenly the demon who was in him began to manifest itself. It was very troubled and said, "Please don't destroy our patron. You have come to destroy it, but please don't leave us without our patron." There's no room for doubt—the devil knows very well who Jesus is, he knew who Paul was, and he knows who we are who harm him. Hallelujah!

We ordered every stall to dry up and not to prosper and decreed a judgment for salvation which would allow those servants held captive by the devil to see their terrible error. We ordered confusion and frustration among the devil's troops and ranks.

We could hardly breathe while walking through that witches' sabbath because of the demonic oppression that lay so heavy everywhere. I saw in the spirit what appeared to be shining giants in the middle of deep darkness. I had been fearful since the night before that the devil would physically appear as he had done in that same place years earlier, when I was involved in magic. I will never forget that experience of seeing the physical manifestation of this ruler of darkness called the Patrono de los Miserables.

I admit that the night before taking the witchcraft market, such memories had made me afraid of a new and wild encounter. I had never been back to the place since that meeting with the devil before my conversion to Christ. Now I was returning with the sword of God in my hand to destroy it. I had to pray a lot to overcome that terrifying memory.

Suddenly those who were outside warned us that the sorcerers were getting organized to attack us and that they had already sacrificed a rooster to counteract what we had come to do. We didn't lose any time. We took the fruit of the vine and poured it out as a drink offering to heal the land and break the covenants.

Once we had broken the covenants, my eyes fell upon an enormous, filthy trash place at the end of the market. There he was, the ruler of darkness himself, with the same tattered clothes he had worn before; but now he was cornered and without strength, bound and unable to speak, totally defeated.

I looked at him without any fear and with deep contempt. I was completely convinced that now we had won. We didn't waste any more time, knowing that the counterattack was being forged and that we had to get out of there as soon as possible. We quickly got into the cars, leaving behind the defeated army of the devil who could do nothing to us. Glory to God!

Two days after this great battle finished, they had to close the streets around the witchcraft market, because all the sorcerers became involved in an unprecedented dispute in which many of them were wounded. We received news that many witches and santeros had come to the feet of Jesus.

We also know that during the second attack we made on this place months later, the chief of the witches fell terminally ill and no magic could heal him. His son was saved—praise God—and was trying to share the gospel with his father, but without any positive outcome. Unfortunately, we eventually heard of his death, too. The point is this: Effective evangelism in areas that have been powerfully taken by the devil can be achieved only through territorial battle.

False Gods of the Aztecs

The main temple of the Aztecs was another place that greatly impacted me during that battle against the pillars of iniquity.

We had made a study of all the gods that had been worshiped in that place and had rebuked them one by one, breaking every covenant that had been made over our nation. There were not many of us. Each commando team had 12 members, with the majority of the soldiers being in the cars driving seven times around the city. So we had only the voices of 12 people in that enormous building, and we knew that we wouldn't make a loud din. Yet, while we were rebuking, a cloud of bats began to form like a great whirlwind, shrieking and disappearing into the sky.

We understood that those animals were a visible manifestation of what was happening in the spiritual realm. But the devil didn't leave things like that. As soon as we had finished praying, two barking dogs that were acting as though they were rabid appeared out of nowhere and came at us.

I knew that those involved in witchcraft believe that an offering has to be made to the devil at the end of every ceremony so as not to hinder the work he has commissioned the good spirits to do. The devil then comes as a dog, which is one of his most ferocious forms of appearance, and eats the offering. This satanic spirit receives the name Exu and is greatly feared and respected among the witches for its fierceness and evil power.

When I saw the enraged dogs, the Lord revealed to me that they were an exact manifestation of this evil spirit. So I rebuked them with all the authority of His name. Instantly the dogs stopped dead in their tracks and ran whining to hide under a wall of planks used for construction.

We also took the Palace of Justice and the president's house. God provided a sister who worked in the president's house, and she anointed the whole place. One month later the president was giving a meal in that building for a thousand evangelical pastors, and for the first time in history, a sermon filled with the Holy Spirit was openly preached in the president's home. Since then there have been radical reforms in the Justice Department, and many corrupt judges have been removed from their positions.

In some places we ask God to make us invisible, because it is sometimes difficult to reach a place guarded by the police. This was the case at the monument of the Niños Heroes (the Child Heroes), also known as the Altar de la Patria (the Altar of the Motherland), and other strategic sites in Teotihuacan.

A Triumphal Entry

Space forbids my telling about everything that happened at each pillar and what the people experienced in each of the cars. You should know, however, that at the end of each morning's circling, all of the war teams met together to pray in the main square of the capital, the central square in Mexico City. Several of us would be in a group waiting for the others (circling Mexico City seven times, even at full speed, takes more than eight hours). We held hands and worshiped God, whose promise had been "You will wipe out the names of their gods from under heaven and nobody will stop you" (see Deut. 7:24). Although we stood in a place bustling with people and traffic, the police did not move in on us; and nobody dared to come near us, much less interrupt us. The Lord was ruling in all His fullness.

We communicated with the cars by means of radio. On the last day the moment drew near, the time we had been waiting for after seven days of prayer and years of oppression. The moment the last cars entered the city's center, we knew the walls of the great stronghold would fall and that God's army would possess the land.

I still remember that moment, and even as I am writing my eyes are filled with tears at the excitement of how incredible those minutes were. In the distance, from Fifth of May Avenue, which meets the square, we began to see the waving flags and signal lights, which to us made the cars shine like chariots of fire. More than in the natural, it was the fire of the glory of God that was over them. They shone like a victory torch which was about to ignite a great fire that would never stop burning in our city. Hundreds of angels entered first, flying over us; and while they fluttered back and forth, we began to hear the sound of the horns and the trumpets of victory.

We were all weeping before the presence of the Holy Spirit. Suddenly, nearly 100 cars entered the square like an armada clothed in the light of Christ. With colored flags and songs of praise, they drove around the square. We were prostrate in worship and jubilee, offering up a new song and every form of exalted expression to God.

The warriors of God got out of their cars and came running with their banners and blazons to join the rest of us. All of us the same Body, one Church, one sound of praise. Then the Lord spoke and said:

Behold, this land will never more be called Mexico, the navel of the world, but MOSHAH-ELOHIM, the place over which my throne is seated.

The place was filled with the glory of God as a shining light; and from that time until now, the gospel has continued to be preached in that square, something that wasn't possible before. God had told us that He would come down from the heavens to break the stronghold and that the earth would shake as a sign, so we were all waiting for the promise to be fulfilled.

The first tremor came at 10 o'clock in the morning. The walls of the stronghold came down so powerfully that the second tremor at seven o'clock in the evening shook not only Mexico but also Egypt, Greece and Taiwan at the same time. The following day the headlines in the daily newspapers on May 22, 1994, read: "WHAT IS HAPPENING? THE WHOLE EARTH SHOOK."

Hallelujah! Glory to God!

Since then many things have happened: Thousands of people are coming to Christ, many traditional churches have received the baptism in the Spirit, and the warfare movement in Mexico is an example for many nations. We have heard the sound of the Lord's trumpet of war, and we will not stop until we see our nation conquered.

Conquering a Mountain

We are taking increasingly stronger and more definitive steps to destroy the spheres of captivity that have imprisoned millions of

Mexicans. Some of them we know could not have been co
quered by any kind of human ability, such as the taking of Mount Popocatepetl. This experience not only changed the lives of those of us who climbed it and took part in the battle, but it brought great changes to our country as well.

At the Mexicans in Victory conference in November 1994, Dr. Rony Chaves said that Popocatepetl would have to be climbed in order to destroy the devil's throne. It was not a coincidence that when Satan heard this, the volcano became active. With Satan thus trying to protect his throne, the task of conquering the mountain seemed impossible. But, as Rony says, "If you want to see what you have never seen, then do what you have never done." So the church began to pray.

One afternoon while returning from Peru, my airplane passed by this large volcano and I heard the voice of the Spirit telling me: *It's time to take it.* Shortly after my return, we began to make the necessary preparations and increased the amount of prayers for taking the mountain. The battle would be difficult, and the throne of darkness was strengthened with fire from the mountain's volcanic activity. We felt that we stood before the gates of hellfire–which was the actual name given to the crater atop Popocatepetl.

This was the most intense prophetic challenge we had undertaken up to that time. The soldiers' lives depended on our spiritual ears hearing the voice of God precisely. To climb an active volcano, which was warned against by volcanologists and prohibited by the authorities, to enter the place where Satan holds the dominion of the ancient god Quetzalcoatl and idolatry, we had to be absolutely sure we had heard the voice of God.

Hundreds of people had been sacrificed on Popocatepetl, giving power to false gods and the gates of hellfire. Year after year, fire is taken from a place in the crater called the Devil's Spine and is brought to burn perpetually before the idol.

One of the tasks of those who worshiped before this demonic throne was to behead men, which today they continue to do secretly in the city of Cholula, at the foot of Popocatepetl. Spiritually speaking, this practice explains the lack of male leadership and the strong matriarchal influence in our country. Millions of Mexicans have been bound by the covenants that have been carried out in this place, and for this reason it was necessary to climb up the volcano to undo them.

Warnings Versus the Voice of God

It was a fierce fight against the lies of the devil. Satan tried to persuade us not to do it by sending volcanologists who told us of all the dangers involved in climbing the volcano. They told us it was shaking 18 times a day with jolts measuring at least 7.0 on the Richter scale, that burning acid was coming out of the ground and that deadly gases were coming through the cracks everywhere. But God told us: *It is time to go up!*

The devil sent us mountaineers, who told us of all the ways we could die in the mountains, from blood-congealing to heart and kidney failure which would kill us on the spot. But we continued to hear God say: *It is time to go up!*

Three days before the climb was scheduled, some pastors from a neighboring town called and asked me to postpone the climb, since it had been reported on the radio that the volcano would erupt on the exact date we had chosen. But God kept saying: *It is time to go up.*

We were denied the governmental permits to enter the cordoned-off area of the mountain. Police patrols put up road blocks, and they closed the road that actually goes up Popocatepetl.

Obviously desperate, the devil sent someone to tell us that a rock group was going to secretly climb the volcano that very day to dedicate their new record to Satan. But God continued saying: *It is time to go up!*

Everything seemed to be against us. The devil had tried to deceive me 15 days earlier by sending a continual stabbing pain in my heart, kidneys and legs. But I knew it wasn't a question of physical condition—first, because God had said *Go up*; and second, because I believed that the power of the Holy Spirit would transport us to the top. There was no other way we would be able to make an ascent of 5,400 meters.

Attacking the Mountain

The day came, and we started climbing at three o'clock in the morning. God had warned us to be careful of the tepehuanes and the shamans. Respectively, these are warrior spirits who care for hills, and sorcerers who are said to be transfigured into animals.

Since the battle was going to be intense, together with the pastors of Puebla we had organized prayer vigils in all the towns on the edge of Popocatepetl. The pastors of Cuernavaca, led by Pastor Jacobo Mondragon and my sister, Mercedes, would drive a caravan of cars around the several volcanoes in the area, breaking every covenant in the surrounding populations and delivering their inhabitants from captivity.

Another group would keep watch from our camp in Paso de Cortes on the side of the volcano, and the last group would do battle in Villa de Guadalupe, breaking the belt of fire that joined the power of Popocatepetl. There was tremendous unity among all the battle teams, and some saw angels taking up their positions to fight.

The climb was obviously grim, with thunder, lightning and hail surrounding us. The presence of the tepehuanes and shamans throughout the forest we passed through gave us goose bumps. We kept on praying and rebuking, while Rony anointed the whole way.

It took us a long time to find a shelter we knew about, which took away the possibility of getting any sleep. At half past three in the morning we left the cabin and continued toward our goal. We bravely prayed for God to remove the police—and a spirit of deep sleep fell on the guards who were blocking access to Tlamacas, located eight kilometers from the volcano and at the point where the ascent begins.

The place was desolate, the patrols had left, and the only light left on was at the guard's hut. Carefully we removed one of the poles that had been stuck into the ground blocking the road. Fortunately, the Lord had shown us that we should have Jeeps waiting on an asphalt road a little farther on, so we could sneak through the barrier on foot and hook up with the vehicles.

We advanced in darkness until we reached the end of the road. Then we got out of our vehicles and began the great battle. It was beautiful to see the army of God. We were all wearing ephods (satin cloth worn over the chest) with the different colors of the Tabernacle and the different names of God written on them in golden letters. On our head were bands of purple ribbons with the words, also in gold, "Holiness to the Lord."

Satan's Counterattacks

Just a few feet after having begun the journey, we were met by a group of bulls which bellowed desperately and were extremely disturbed. We attacked the spirits of the shamans and continued.

However, that was only the first attack. Simultaneously Rony and I felt strong chest pains as though our hearts were going to explode. One of the pastors, along with two other sisters, felt from the Lord they should keep watch below and not go up. This was a great blessing, since they covered the group with prayer.

Then came one of the attacks the Lord had warned would come from Iztlaccihuatl, the volcano of the sleeping bride that lies near Popocatepetl, her bridegroom. In a vision the Lord showed us a woman with a bleeding face and carrying a beating heart in her hand. She was asking for our hearts; but we knew that the only power the devil has is to deceive us, so in spite of the intense pain in our chests, we carried on.

This was a thorn in the flesh we had to fight throughout the whole journey. Satan would not cease from telling us that we were too old and that our hearts would fail at any moment. Certainly our faith was tested to the utmost; but the voice of God, which was far stronger, drove us on.

All along the way we found figures of every kind of serpent, altars and an enormous diabolical throne made out of two enormous rocks that are commonly known as the devil's teeth. We were stalked on every side by the two terrible guardian spirits, Talcaelel and Calibuz. At times a spirit of fear tried to intimidate us. Rony crossed out the number 666, which was symbolically engraved on rocks along the way. As we went, we worshiped and asked God to give us strength for the climb. It truly was a strong challenge, especially because of the loose ash our feet sank into, making the climb heavy going.

Dragon at Dawn

The dawn was glorious, as though an awakening of a great victory over our country was being signed in the skies as an indelible covenant. We were filled with great joy. To the north the sleeping woman, Iztlaccihuatl, was clothed in tremendous, challenging majesty, completely covered with snow. The hem of her clothes seemed to be edged with the morning mist that surrounded her skirts. In the distance, the mountain Pico de Orizaba and the volcano of the Malinche kept vigil like two watchmen on their towers, not missing the slightest movement of the armies that were recruited on top of the firmament.

We also perceived what God had prophesied to us: the archangel Michael and his angels had been enlisted for combat. We could feel their strength all about us.

Meanwhile, the convoy of cars had departed to make the 500-kilometer trip around the area's volcanoes. All the cars were adorned with unfurled flags with Scripture verses of battle on them and had their signal lights on. On several stretches of the roadway, God allowed them to see His warhorse galloping ahead of them.

Halfway up the volcano we split up, destroying the altars where a large number of sacrifices had been made. Rony continued going straight up. When we had finished tearing down those powers and breaking those covenants, there was an earthquake we felt must have registered at least 7.0 on the Richter scale. The whole volcano shook and roared from within. It was truly impressive.

As we climbed, the wind picked up violently to the point where we had to use our ice axes, sticking them into the ground so we wouldn't be blown away by the strong gusts. It felt like the lava stirring in the center of the volcano was grumbling under our feet. Above us, the fumarole—the central hole from which lava and gases poured—was spewing the volcano's fiery contents with all its strength. In fact, we later learned that the volcanologist's apparatus reported strong fumarolic and telluric activity that very day.

We climbed as if we were being transported by a horse of fire with great speed and energy, just making stops short enough to catch our breath. Suddenly, right before us, there appeared a gigantic dragon as if made out of the cloud that filled the width of the crater. However, we could soon see that it wasn't an actual cloud since it remained static for 20 minutes without losing any of its form. In the middle of a tempestuous gale, the fire and gases from the fumarole bent in such a way that it came out practically horizontal and disappeared toward the southeast.

When we saw the dragon, we covered ourselves with the blood of Jesus and began to do battle against it. Its face was directed toward the place where Rony was, along with three other men who had reached the crater, and a kind of white fire came out of its mouth. The Lord gave us instructions to raise our hands and to prophesy that shining rays would come forth from our hands. We did this in faith, even though we didn't see the rays. What is marvelous is the fact that later we learned that below, in Paso de Cortes, not only did warriors there see the dragon, but they also saw many rays coming from where we were and wounding the dragon. Those in the cars also testified that they had seen many rays directed toward the crater at the exact time this had happened.

To see this manifestation was not only impacting, but it also coincided with the first covenant made in the volcano's crater. Historians relate that the first person to climb to the volcano was Chalchihuitzin, a priest of the god Mixcohuatl, the cloud serpent. He was seeking to bring rain, since there had been a great drought; and he whipped himself on the edge of the crater as a sacrifice to his deity.

The battle intensified more when Rony took the arrows we had brought to the summit and anointed them with oil, thrusting them into the ground at the edge of the crater. Guided by the

Holy Spirit, we decreed that they split the devil's neck. Rony then removed the arrows, and one of the four men who had reached the inside edge of the crater took the arrows and shot them at the dragon, prophesying its total destruction. At that moment the ground began to practically boil under their feet, and they saw an enormous number of flames come up from the ground. A cloud of sulfur began to suffocate them. God spoke to them, telling them to get down; then a second earthquake started. Rony then prophesied that what had been taken by the devil for so long would now be called the Mount of Zion.

Meanwhile, another team and I continued to climb another path with great enthusiasm. When we saw the cloud of the dragon's head turn toward us, I shouted with all my strength at that very moment: "We have overcome by the blood of the Lamb and the word of our testimony as we have denied our lives unto death!"

Suddenly six more dragons materialized in a black cloud that came up out of the ground and headed straight for us. The lack of oxygen and the demonic oppression were suffocating. We fought with all the power and authority of Jesus Christ, prophesying the Word of God and extending our hands over the dragons so that the rays of power from God would destroy them. We also confessed they could not touch us, because we were hidden in Christ. When they were just about on top of us, the hand of God broke them up into thousands of pieces.

We still hadn't finished, however. At the bottom of the valley the great volcano Iztlaccihuatl lifted its head as if being armed with great power to defend her beloved Popocatepetl, just as the legend states. All around the snow-covered sleeping woman, as she is also called, an enormous army of black shadows with humanoid form were being launched against us. Although the clouds were being carried along by the wind at great speed, these black silhouettes didn't move.

We raised up an invisible wall between the two volcanoes and ourselves and charged forward, prophesying that the fire of God would consume them. Intense heat came from the sky, and within 10 minutes all of the snow on Iztlaccihuatl had melted. We were told that never before had the volcano been seen without snow. Fire also descended on Popocatepetl, and the remaining snow there began to rapidly melt. The thaw formed two turbulent rivers which God kept us from so that we would be able to cross over without any danger on the return.

Orders to Descend

Some 100 meters from the peak, Rony appeared on one side of the volcano and ordered us to stop our ascent and to start going down immediately. I have to admit this was probably one of the hardest orders of obedience that I have had to respect in my Christian walk, because I was only a few steps from the crater and I wanted with all my being to reach that destination. My heart was broken with frustration, but I knew that there must have been a powerful reason why Rony had given this order. I knew it was his desire as well mine that I reach the crater. With utmost pain, I instructed my team to descend, and I took the first step back down.

While this was happening, the convoy of cars led by my sister and Jacobo Mondragon made the long trip, taking the villages (they prayed for 400 towns and cities). All along the way, churches were waiting for them with great joy in the Spirit, and more cars kept joining the great caravan. Some of the pastors of the Alliance Church in Puebla also joined in fighting the battle after having spent the whole night praying and watching.

One of the experiences worth mentioning occurred when the caravan arrived at Izucar de Matamoros. When they arrived, the church was shut up. The pastor had been trying to evangelize the area for 45 years without much success. It was explained to them that in that town there were more than 200 brothels and that the level of violence in the city was such that not even the government could guarantee the safety of its inhabitants. The pastor had been left paralyzed, with his faith dying.

The war contingent then entered the small, abandoned church, with some 100 warriors in full spiritual battle. The pastor couldn't believe it. To him it was like a dream in which the answer from heaven had finally come. They broke all the demonic covenants; they rebuked the pastor's paralysis and together with a few local members, they praised the Lord and touched the shofars, or rams' horns, as a sign of victory. Something powerful happened in that place, and the pastor will never be the same.

Back at the mountain, we realized that the battle was won when a seal of it in the form of an eagle appeared out of nowhere and flew above the volcano, releasing God's presence on all of us.

When we reached the place called Las Cruces, we broke all the covenants of idolatry and matriarchy which ruled over that place. Later, we all took off the ephods and each one of us, decreeing a prophecy over Mexico, tossed them to the ground. We then covered them with 12 stones, anointed them and worshiped God, consecrating the volcano for His glory. Those who were below saw an enormous white dove fluttering at the top of the volcano. The victory had been won. When we came down, all the warriors from the different states were waiting for us, rejoicing. A little later the caravan of cars arrived, with warriors blowing trumpets and a ram's horn. We all gave thanks to God and shouted in worship seven shabachs of triumph. It was a very exciting moment that was obviously filled with the Holy Spirit.

Although everyone was joyful, in truth I was still a little frustrated from not being allowed to reach the crater. But I handed it over to God and decided to rejoice like the others. The following day after having taken Rony to the airport, I took a siesta to regain some of my lost strength. While I slept, the Lord transported me in the spirit to the moment when I was reaching the summit. I was shouting to the devil, "We have overcome you by the blood of the Lamb and by the word of our testimony, having denied our lives unto death." Then I saw myself sadly taking the first step back down in obedience to the authority over me. I heard the voice of the Spirit telling me: *Daughter, I want you to see what happened when you took that step of submission to my prophet.*

I was then shown an enormous and abominable woman positioned between the dragon and myself. In that moment when my feet took the first step down, the hand of God squeezed the abomination between His fingers, shattering her into thousands of pieces. The Holy Spirit added,

> *This woman represented the power of the matriarch over Mexico, and your obedience was what destroyed it. This power had been established by the Jezabelic rulership of la Malinche, who dominated and subjugated all the Indians and took freedom away from man, setting herself up as sovereign. Here the legal right of matriarchy was established over your country by a Mexican woman. Now I am destroying this covenant through a Mexican woman. For this reason it was necessary that only the four men reach the top.*

The Lord continued,

> *They were four symbolic men. The first symbolized God's government over the earth; the second, leadership in the*

Church; the third, leadership in the nation; and the fourth, leadership in the home.

At the same time, my sister, Mercedes, received a word from Zechariah 3:8: "Listen, O high priest Joshua and your associates seated before you, who are *men* symbolic of things to come: I am going to bring my servant, the Branch" (emphasis added). My mourning turned to joy as I realized that my obedience had been a part of God's plan to restore male leadership to the area.

We had climbed the mountain on May 22, the Day of Ce Malinali. My elation became even greater when I researched the Aztec calendar and discovered that Malinche, who had originated the covenants that robbed the area of male leadership, was named after the very day on which we conquered the mountain!

I close this account of the beautiful victory that God, through His grace, gave us, with the word the Lord gave to the warriors who fought in Paso de Cortes between the two volcanoes:

The day of the LORD is near for all nations. As you have done, it will be done to you; your deeds will return upon your own head. Just as you drank on my holy hill, so all the nations will drink continually; they will drink and drink and be as if they had never been. But on Mount Zion will be deliverance; it will be holy, and the house of Jacob will possess its inheritance. The house of Jacob will be a fire and the house of Joseph a flame; the house of Esau will be stubble, and they will set it on fire and consume it. There will be no survivors from the house of Esau. The Lord has spoken. Deliverers will go up on Mount Zion to govern the mountains of Esau. And the kingdom will be the LORD's (Obad. 1:15-18,21).

EPILOGUE

GOD IS MUSTERING AN ARMY!

Today the call of God goes out as it did in the oracle God gave the prophet Isaiah against the evil nation of Babylon:

> Raise a banner on a bare hilltop, shout to them; beckon to them to enter the gates of the nobles. I have commanded my holy ones; I have summoned my warriors to carry out my wrath—those who rejoice in my triumph. Listen, a noise on the mountains, like that of a great multitude! Listen, an uproar among the kingdoms, like nations massing together! The LORD Almighty is mustering an army for war (Isa. 13:2-4).

You may have read this book and felt this divine summons in your own heart. God is calling for soldiers, and you may be among those who can respond, with Isaiah, "Here am I. Send me!" (Isa. 6:8). Yet you may also fear that you are untrained and even unworthy of this challenge.

I believe it is important for all those who initiate the aggressive kind of territorial warfare recommended in this book to know that every great strategy has begun by someone simply *believing.*

Sometimes we think we need to be great ministers to start something, but that is not the case. God does not need an expert to begin a work. He needs *believers*, people of faith who believe that He can do anything and that His work depends on Him and not on man.

It is true that we are at the beginning of a move of warfare the likes of which we have never seen before. The prophetic mantle that is descending upon the face of the earth is like nothing that has ever been seen before. We are the pioneers of a new power and a new revelation of the Holy Spirit.

For many, anything new prompts fear. They prefer to wait and see what others will do before they become involved. Amen. What is important is that they get involved, not when they get involved.

This has been the pattern throughout history. Brave people who understood that they had received something from the Holy Spirit acted by faith and made it reality. People of previous moves often opposed them, believing that what they received was sufficient. We see this with water baptism, with the outpouring of the Holy Spirit on Azusa Street, with speaking in tongues, with the gifts of the Spirit, with deliverance ministries, with dance and the arts and now with territorial warfare. All these movements had pioneers, and all of them had their opponents.

As Dr. Rony Chaves says, quoting Don Quixote: "The dogs are barking, Sancho. It's a sign that we are riding!"

If we really fear God, He will keep us from making mistakes. If we are exercised in prayer and in silence where His voice is heard, He will lead us. But we always have to remember that "from the days of John the Baptist until now, the kingdom of heaven has been forcefully advancing, and forceful men lay hold of it" (Matt. 11:12).

Public and Private Soldiers

We need to understand that even those of us who may not be called to take the lead in spiritual warfare of a public nature can often be invaluable to the Lord behind the scenes. Some of God's battles take place in the light and are seen by everyone. Others, however, are God's secret; and perhaps you are called to be one of the behind-the-scenes planners and strategists in this great battle.

All of us know about the glory and splendor of Solomon's magnificent Temple. Great people of the earth saw his kingdom and greatness. But behind this marvel was a simple shepherd boy who had entered into God's secrets—a shepherd boy who became a king.

It was David, the man after God's own heart, who planned the Temple in which his son Solomon gloried. It was David who knew and lived in intimacy with God, who had a heart with the vision of building a sublime house for the God of glory and who had the friendship and love of God to enter into His chambers of wisdom and to draw from them the perfect plans for the Temple.

"'All this,' David said, 'I have in writing from the hand of the LORD upon me, and he gave me understanding in all the details of the plan'" (1 Chron. 28:19). Although David had attained everything–the gold, the silver, the bronze, the iron, the wood, the precious stones, the marble in abundant quantity for the construction of the Temple–he also had the humility to give over the visible work to his son. Who is of greater esteem in the eyes of God? The one who ordered the bricks to be laid or the one who received the blueprints from the hands of the Most High?

God is raising up a remnant all over the earth, a glorious army of deep intercession and territorial warfare, a people of divine choice, just as God chose David. Whether generals or privates in this great army, God needs men and women who hear His trumpet call to battle and who can fight in the confidence that their King has already won the victory. God needs an army that knows with its entire being that they are more than conquerors in Jesus Christ, an army which walks and moves not by sight but by faith, a remnant who have completely opened up their lives and hearts to the Lord, just as Jesus revealed to John.

> Here I am! I stand at the door and knock. If anyone hears my voice and opens the door, I will come in and eat with him, and he with me. To him who overcomes, I will give the right to sit with me on my throne, just as I overcame and sat down with my Father on his throne (Rev. 3:20,21).

The government of the nations is not in the hand of wicked rulers but in the Lord's throne over the nations. "He who has an ear, let him hear what the Spirit says to the churches" (Rev. 2:7).

Intercession and territorial warfare will give birth to a revival the likes of which has never been seen on the earth. Many evangelists will go out and win perhaps millions of souls. Others will found large churches, congregations so large they won't even fit into stadiums. But those who will really have the destiny of the nations in their hands are the ones who will enter the heart of God as David did and will draw the plans and designs from His secret chambers.

The battle is not an end in and of itself. It is the door that unleashes the rivers of life from God's throne. It is what breaks the structures and spheres of captivity so that evangelists can win souls. The battle squadrons are an extension of God's hands to release His dominion on the earth.

A Prayer of Victory and Gratitude

I want to conclude this call to arms with a personal victory prayer for you:

> *I bow my knees that in this hour the Spirit of revelation and the knowledge of God would come upon you, that the prophetic mantle and the mantle of spiritual warfare would descend on you now, that a new dimension of deep prayer would be released in your life, and above all that fellowship with God and the ability to hear His voice with all clarity would be granted to you by the Holy Spirit. I also praise and glorify Jesus Christ for having given me the privilege of writing this book and for the wonderful hours of fellowship I have had with Him. I infinitely thank the Holy Spirit for having put so many marvelous experiences before me that have not only changed my life but also that of the Church that God has given to us. To Jesus be all the glory, power, majesty and praise. Amen.*

APPENDIX

THE RELIGION OF SANTERIA

Santeria (pronounced *san-ter-EE-a*) Santeria is an ancient pagan religion that originated in the Yoruba tribe of West Africa and was brought to the Caribbean region by the slave trade. It is based on the worship of the god Olorun, or Olodumare, who is believed to be the source of *ashe* (*ash-AY*), thought to be the spiritual energy that courses through all that is in the universe, both living and material. Santeria is therefore among the animistic religions of the world, believing that spirits indwell rocks and trees as well as animals and humans.

Followers of Santeria believe that the god Olorun interacts with the world through emissaries called *orishas.* These are spirits who rule over every force of nature and every aspect of human life. It is thought that these spirits can be contacted through magic and sacrifice.

In parts of Latin America where a syncretistic blend of Catholicism and pagan religious practices has flourished, these spirits are often identified with specific Catholic saints. Santeria believers call on them for guidance and blessing, contacting the orishas through rituals that include prayer, divination and *ebo*, or sacrifices (including animals). The rituals may involve song, rhythmic dances and trances.

Santeria is said to be gaining members in the Caribbean, Central and South America, France, the Netherlands and the southern United States.

Significant Spirits to Be Rebuked

These are the most important spirits in Santeria according to their hierarchical order:

- Eleugua, or legbas, a spirit linked with the Holy Child of Atocha, is a warrior spirit who is thought to rule over all the rest.
- Yemaya, linked with the Virgin of Guadalupe and the Virgin of the Lakes, always works accompanied by Elegua; together, the two make up the principality which governs the rest.
- Shango is linked with Santa Barbara, a high warrior spirit who is identified with fire and violence.
- Ochung is linked with the Virgin of Caridad del Cobre.
- Oya is linked with Santa Teresita of the Baby Jesus. This is the spirit of death.

- Obatala is the lord of the serpents and is worshiped as San Lazaro.
- Erzulli is linked with the Sacred Heart of Jesus.
- The Patron of the Wretched is the spirit of poverty and tragedy.
- Exu is the spirit in charge of collecting the offerings for the acts of witchcraft and ceremonies of Santeria. It manifests itself as a dog.
- Loas are unclean spirits that accompany the spirits of Santo and warrior spirits, who are ranked in hierarchical orders.
- Ogun is linked with Saint Peter.
- San Martin Caballero is the saint who is called upon to prosper business.
- San Jorge is a spirit of power and the lord of vampires. He robs the will and strength of his victims.
- San Judas Tadeo is the saint of impossible causes.